Scott Bornstein's

MEMORY TECHNIQUES for VOCABULARY MASTERY

Bornstein Memory Training Schools • Los Angeles

ACKNOWLEDGMENTS

I wish to acknowledge and thank the following people:

Shani Horowitz for her impeccable insight in designing the cover of this book; Ben Vincent for his stimulating, creative and fun illustrations used throughout; Laura Bornstein and Lorilee Moore for their invaluable service in the typing, editing and proofreading of the final manuscript; and particular appreciation to my father, Arthur Bornstein, and my mother for their years of experience and their total support, commitment and encouragement to me on this project.

Second Printing 1984
ISBN 0-9602610-1-X (H)
ISBN 0-9602610-2-8 (S)

Inquiries should be addressed to
Bornstein Memory Training Schools,
11693 San Vicente Blvd., West LosAngeles, California.

Printed in the United States of America

CONTENTS

To my wife, Shani

The most special person I've ever
known, my inspiration, and the
greatest joy of my life.

INTRODUCTION

Have you ever had the frustrating experience of learning new material for school or work only to draw a blank when trying to recall the information?

It doesn't have to be that way. The purpose of this book is to give you confidence in your ability to remember words and their meanings on the occasions when you want to be able to best express yourself. And if you take the time to complete the vocabulary exercises presented here, your retention of all kinds of material will measurably improve.

Although more self-improvement books have been written about vocabulary improvement than almost any other topic, the approach in this book is unique. This is the first book designed exclusively to help you improve your memory for vocabulary. Memory and vocabulary are invariably linked. You must have a strong memory to develop a thorough vocabulary, and knowledge of vocabulary is the foundation for helping you to remember even more vocabulary.

The new vocabulary you acquire will result from the memory methods you learn from this book. Your progress will be a by-product of training your mind to work in a wholly new fashion. And if you invest the short time it takes to learn the techniques, you'll carry the benefits with you the rest of your life.

Research shows the larger a person's vocabulary, the greater potential he or she has for success. Why is it that on such standardized tests as the SAT, GRE, and MCAT, approximately 50% of your score is based on vocabulary? Simply because language ability determines how quickly you'll grasp new concepts and factual information. And in business, law, medicine—in all professions, in fact—the knowledge of relevant vocabulary is critical for entering a given field.

From the earliest age, children are classified according to how "bright" they are, that is, how talkative or how intelligently they use words in a given subject. Once they enter school, it can be readily observed that the "A" students are already familiar with the vocabulary of the subject. Other students, however, spend so much time learning the terminology of a topic that they have little time remaining to learn the subject itself. It is these students who need additional language learning tools to give them the competitive edge.

When using this book you will see full-page illustrations of abstract words and learn how to make associations between words and their meanings. Enjoy these illustrations; they are designed to stimulate your imagination and reinforce methods of association. When you think back to the picture, the word and its meaning will tie together in your memory. All you have to do is create vivid pictures in your mind—the stronger the impression, the longer you will remember the association.

The pictures you learn today, when reviewed tomorrow, will help you to transfer that information into the long-term computer of your mind. The more words you begin to use from this book, the greater ease you'll experience in recalling these words and their meanings.

HOW YOUR MEMORY WORKS

The human mind has fascinated man for centuries. The Greek philosopher Aristotle studied the way the mind records and stores information and called this his "Laws of Logic and Reason." His basic theory was that the new information we learn is related to some idea we already know, usually through similarity of sight or sound.

Memory is, according to one dictionary definition, "the information storage unit of the mind, or a computer." There is a strong similarity between the human mind and a computer in that information stored in the brain may be recalled by a predesignated cue.

Have you experienced hearing someone tell a joke, only to be reminded of another joke yourself? This happens because a word or a phrase in the other person's joke acted as a cue that caused the computer-like functions in your mind to open a "file drawer" under that subject.

The same involuntary process causes your mind to wander during a lecture or when you are reading a book. Since our minds record thoughts or ideas, not individual words, the average person cannot read fast enough to keep the mind from wandering. And no one talks as fast as the mind can think.

This distraction process can be used to advantage when learning new material. Controlling these automatic associations can help you relate words read or spoken to an idea or picture you already know, which will ensure recall at a later date. Vocabulary mastery will allow you to gain the necessary control over your memory to accomplish your goal—an enlarged vocabulary.

A WORD IS WORTH A THOUSAND PICTURES

Your mental computer uses your eyes like the lens of a camera to take pictures of objects that you see. The more vivid the picture you conjure, the longer you remember the association. The visual memory is the strongest area of the memory process. When I ask you to visualize the house you grew up in as a child, you can *see* it—see the houses on the same street, see the elementary school you attended; you actually can see these pictures flash clearly to mind!

The first technique to be learned in memory and vocabulary improvement is to look for the *visualness* in the word itself. Next we *associate* the word to its definition. To associate literally means to bring together and connect two ideas in such a way that they will always be remembered as that same pair of ideas in the future. Think of the first idea, the second comes flashing to mind, and the second idea brings back the first.

Next, observe that vocabulary words can be organized into three categories: (1) visual word/abstract definition; (2) abstract word/visual definition; and (3) abstract word/abstract definition. The category in which the word and its definition occur will determine the method used to record it in your mind. In many cases, logic and reasoning will apply, but in the instances of abstract words or definitions you will learn how to use your imagination to create an association between the word and its meaning.

For instance, you see the word *flag*—which means "to droop"—for the first time. When you see the word flag, you picture a flag that's drooping. (See page 103 for illustration.) What if you saw the word *saturnine*, which means "gloomy"? If you look at the word, you should see a word that you know within the word—Saturn. Think of Saturn as a gloomy planet. (See page 223 for illustration.)

If the word isn't visual, you can listen to the sound of the word to develop an association. In the word *rabid*—which means "angry"—you can hear the word rabbit, and you can visualize an angry rabbit pounding its paw on the ground. (See page 43 for illustration.)

Another approach would be to look at the meaning of the word for something visual to associate with it. For example, *specter* means "ghost". A ghost is visual enough, and if you use a little imagination, and ask yourself whether there is anything familiar in the sound of the word, you should notice that *specter* sounds like *inspector*. Have you ever seen a ghost inspector? (See page 13 for illustration.)

What if you see a word that is not visual and its meaning is not either? This is when we use our most creative mental powers. If you wanted to learn that *eschew* means "to avoid," can you picture "a shoe" being thrown at you and you duck to "avoid" it? (See page 79 for illustration.)

Use logic and observation in making your associations. If you see the word *rotund*, which means "round," what do you notice about the word? Cover up the letter "t" and rotund and round are spelled the same. You can use spelling as another guide to making associations, but you should always use what works best for you. Your mental pictures are the key to success.

Your association can be an amusing story, a picture, an experience, whatever is most effective. Get involved in making connections between the word and its definition and you're on your way to improving your memory in many subjects while enlarging the number of words at your command.

HOW TO MAKE THIS BOOK WORK FOR YOU

In the opening sections of this book, I offer the associations for you to help you get started. You will find that by spending 10 to 15 minutes a day, you will learn memory techniques that will open doors to a new and larger vocabulary.

The first 15 sections of the book will introduce you to memory training—while stimulating your mind with fresh and exciting mental habits. Additional sections give you the vocabulary words and definitions with which to lay the groundwork for your own associations. In each section you will see an example of how each word is used and learn 20 words.

Also, you will learn three word roots, and see six sample words that contain the root you've just learned. Study these word roots and you will learn to recognize hundreds of other words on sight. Like pieces of a puzzle, knowledge of Greek and Latin roots, prefixes, and suffixes will allow you to automatically translate and understand many new words.

Experience has taught me that it is important to review the words you have learned within 24 hours. Check the next day to see if the pictures are still clear in your mind. If they're clear tomorrow, they'll be clear in your mind a week later. Use the words regularly and they will always be there when you need them. In fact, you may want to make 3 x 5 flash cards to carry with you, and quiz yourself throughout the day. The more often you review, the sooner you will *know* the words.

To master vocabulary, continue to have fun learning with your newly discovered memory techniques. Enjoy this book—I loved writing it!

— Scott Bornstein

cache (kash)—hiding place
See your **cash** in the safe **hiding place**.

EXAMPLE OF USE

1. The squirrel found a safe **cache** for his food in the hollow of the tree.
2. To **assuage** his guilt, he apologized profusely and offered to take her out to dinner.
3. There was an **altercation** over whose job it was to lock up the building.
4. He always said he was a pacifist, but when his sister was threatened, he turned **bellicose**.
5. It is probably not a good idea to **brandish** a stick when trying to make friends with a wild animal.
6. The earthquake was a **cataclysm** of unequaled magnitude.
7. The **noisome** odor issuing from the apartment prompted neighbors to call the police.
8. Although the water contains bacteria, they are **innocuous**, and the water is safe to drink.
9. I'll have some lemonade to **slake** my thirst.
10. In spite of fierce opposition to his argument, he clung **tenaciously** to his original point.
11. Some people say that he does so little work, he's really just a **sinecure** around the office.
12. If the tree looks **truncated**, it's because we had to trim a branch before it caused damage to the house.
13. Santa Claus is traditionally portrayed as a **rotund**, bearded gentleman.
14. Cynics say that students are **apathetic** to every school problem except the parking problem.
15. The actor was blessed with a **largess** of talent.
16. Hamlet stated his **dilemma** in the soliloquy that begins, "To be or not to be . . . ."
17. We have **plumbed** the depths of the sea and discovered pollution everywhere.
18. To protect its reputation, the company agreed to **redress** the error its billing department made.
19. After the American Civil War, it was unconstitutional for one man to hold another in **thrall**.
20. In the interests of **verity**, I wish you'd tell us what you really saw.

Man does not live by words alone, despite the fact that sometimes he has to eat them.
—Adlai Stevenson

WORD	DEFINITION	ASSOCIATION
1. **cache** (kash) n.	hiding place	See your **cash** in the safe-**hiding place**.
2. **assuage** (a-swayj) v.	to calm, make less severe	To **massuage** someone, **calms** and **relieves** pain.
3. **altercation** (awl-ter-kay-shon) n.	argument, quarrel or dispute	See an **argument** over the clothes **alteration**.
4. **bellicose** (beli-kohs) adj.	warlike	Ring **bells** on the **coast** to announce **war**.
5. **brandish** (bran-dish) v.	shake or wave menacingly	**Shake** and **wave** a **brandy** bottle over a **dish.**
6. **cataclysm** (kat-a-kliz-em) n.	violent upheaval	See the two **cats** having a **collision** (cat-a-collision).
7. **noisome** (noi-som) adj.	offensive, harmful odor	Does the **smell** of a skunk **annoy-some**?
8. **innocuous** (i-nok-yoo-us) adj.	harmless	An **innocent** person is **harmless.**
9. **slake** (slayk) v.	quench, satisfy	See yourself at the **lake—quenching** and **satisfying** your thirst.
10. **tenacious** (te-nay-shus) adj.	hold fast, persistence	See the **tennis-shoes holding fast**.
11. **sinecure** (si-ne-kyoor) n.	an official position—well paid with little to do	You're so **well paid** and **secure**, it's a **sin**!
12. **truncate** (trung-kayt) v.	to shorten by cutting off	**Cut** the **trunk** off the **gate**.
13. **rotund** (roh-tund) adj.	round	**Rotund** spells **round** without the **"t"**.
14. **apathy** (ap-a-thee) n.	lack of interest	See a **path** with people on it who **don't care**.
15. **largess** (lahr-zhes) n.	innate generosity	See a very **large** and **generous** man.
16. **dilemma** (di-lem-a) n.	difficult situation	**Emma** ate a **dill** pickle and is in a **mess**.
17. **plumb** (plum) v.	to test, measure	Mom squeezes every **plum** in the store **to test** and **measure** them.
18. **redress** (ri-dres) v.	set right again	Let me **re-dress** you **right** this time.
19. **thrall** (thrawl) n.	slave	**They're all** my **slaves**.
20. **verity** (ver-i-tee) n.	truth	I want to **verify** the **truth**.

ego—I
"Wherever **ego's, I** go."

WORD ROOT	MEANING	ASSOCIATION
EGO	**I**	Wherever **ego's, I** go.
ego (ee-gho) n.	the self.	
egotist (ee-goh-tist) n.	one who talks too much about himself.	
egoistic (ee-goh-is-tik) n.	self-centeredness.	
egomaniac (ee-goh-may-ni-ak) n.	quality or state of being extremely self-centered.	
super ego (soo-per ee-goh) n.	a person's ideals for himself.	
egocentric (ee-goh-sen-trik) adj.	self-centered.	
PRIM, PRIMER	**first**	**Primer** is the **first** coat of paint used.
prime (prym) adj.	chief, most important.	
prima ballerina (pree-ma bal-e-ree-na) n.	the chief female dancer in a ballet.	
primeval (pry-mee-val) adj.	of the earliest time in the world.	
primitive (prim-i-tive) adj.	early stage of civilization.	
primordial (pry-mor-di-al) adj.	same as primeval.	
primer (prim-er) n.	first elementary textbook.	
MONO, MON	**one**	**Monday** is my # **one** day.
monotony (mo-not-o-nee) n.	boring due to lack of variety.	
monologue (mon-o-lawg) n.	long speech by one person.	
monochromatic (mon-oh-kroh-mat-ik) adj.	of one color only.	
monocle (mon-o-kel) n.	eyeglass for one eye only.	
monogamy (mo-nog-a-mee) n.	system of marriage to one person.	
monarchy (mon-ar-kee) n.	form of government where ruler is king, queen or emperor.	

REVIEW

Draw a line between the word and its correct definition.

1. **sinecure**	a. to measure
2. **largess**	b. slave
3. **redress**	c. truth
4. **truncate**	d. difficult situation
5. **thrall**	e. lack of interest
6. **dilemma**	f. round
7. **apathy**	g. to set right again
8. **verity**	h. innate generosity
9. **rotund**	i. a position requiring little work
10. **plumb**	j. to shorten or abbreviate

Circle the correct word below each definition.

1. **hiding place**
   (miscreant, hiatus, cache, gambol)
2. **to calm**
   (portend, assuage, obfuscate, accrue)
3. **a dispute**
   (altercation, gamut, quandry, panacea)
4. **warlike**
   (germane, mellifluous, bellicose, hirsute)
5. **to shake menacingly**
   (brandish, rescind, undulate, quell)
6. **violent upheaval**
   (sycophant, chagrin, pilaster, cataclysm)
7. **offensive**
   (placid, mundane, noisome, blatant)
8. **harmless**
   (loquacious, innocuous, lachrymal, sonorous)
9. **to satisfy**
   (slake, feign, malinger, ameliorate)
10. **to be persistent**
    (nugatory, restive, tenacious, dogmatic)
11. **self-centered**
    (monogamy, primordial, egocentric, neophyte)
12. **government with one ruler**
    (monologue, misogynist, monarchy, moribund)
13. **early stage of civilization**
    (primitive, genetic, proboscis, pusillanimous)

2

specter (spek-ter)—ghost

See the ghost **inspecter** looking for **ghosts**!

EXAMPLE OF USE

1. Shakespeare's Hamlet is moved to action by the presence of his father's **specter.**

2. He treats her rudely, which is an **affront** to her dignity.

3. He was lucky to get a suspended sentence for **abetting** the commission of a felony.

4. We **bandied** words back and forth for a half-hour, then concentrated on the movie we were supposed to be watching.

5. To **allay** the child's fears, the doctor calmly explained what he was going to do.

6. One of the **ironies** of our democratic system of government is that we treasure our freedom to vote, yet only a small percentage actually make use of that freedom.

7. In this sentence, the proofreader used a **caret** to indicate that the word "very" goes before "cold."

8. I **ransacked** my room, but still can't find that library book that's overdue.

9. We had to **fabricate** a story to explain why we were late for class.

10. The lawyer **gulled** the witness into a confession.

11. One of the contributing factors to the American Revolution was the tea tax **levied** by the British on the colonies.

12. Justice is not always **meted** out fairly, according to the critics of our courts.

13. The minister, **missal** in hand, asked the congregation to join him in prayer.

14. These wildflowers will make a pretty **nosegay**.

15. Certain prominent people may be called **mavericks** when they try to make their own rules.

16. Joggers should be aware that there are exercises for strengthening the **hamstring** muscles.

17. There is an air of **piety** in this church.

18. The babysitter **hoodwinked** the children into drinking their milk by giving them spoons and telling them it was dessert.

19. We'll have to **curtail** today's lesson because this room will be needed for a meeting in twenty minutes.

20. When asked if he'd mind working overtime, John made a **wry** face.

Add 1800 more words to your vocabulary and you can graduate from the ordinary to the superior.
—John H. Steadman

WORD	DEFINITION	ASSOCIATION
1. **specter** (spek-ter) n.	ghost	See the ghost **inspecter** looking for **ghosts**!
2. **affront** (a-frunt) v.	insult deliberately	She **insultingly** slammed **a front** door in his face.
3. **abet** (a-bet) v.	to aid or encourage in wrongdoing	He needed some **courage,** which was **wrong** to place **a bet**.
4. **bandy** (ban-dee) v.	to pass to and fro, exchange remarks in quarreling	See two people **exchanging** wedding **bands** and having a **quarrel**.
5. **allay** (a-lay) v.	to calm	**I lay** down and feel very **calm**.
6. **irony** (i-ro-nee) n.	words that are opposite of what was intended	I **ironed** my **knee,** which was **opposite of what I intended**!
7. **caret** (kar-it) n.	an omission mark: "it is missing" ^	The **carrot** with a **mark** is **missing** from my lunch.
8. **ransack** (ran-sak) v.	search thoroughly	He **ran** into the **sack** and **searched** it thoroughly.
9. **fabricate** (fab-ri-kayt) v.	to construct, invent	I need the **fabric** to **construct** the dress.
10. **gull** (gul) v.	to trick, deceive	See the sea **gull** performing a magic **trick.**
11. **levy** (lev-ee) v.	to impose or collect a tax or fine	You must pay extra **tax** on those **levi** jeans.
12. **mete** (meet) v.	to distribute, to allot	See **a lot** of **meat** being **distributed**.
13. **missal** (mis-al) n.	book containing prayers used in the Mass	The **prayer books** are put in the **missle** after **Mass**.
14. **nosegay** (nohz-gay) n.	small bouquet of flowers	Put your **nose** in a **gay bouquet** of **flowers.**
15. **maverick** (mav-e-rik) n.	unbranded calf or other young animal	**My Rick** stopped the **wild, unbranded calves.**
16. **hamstring** (ham-string) n.	tendon behind the knee	Tie the **ham** with **string behind** the **knee.**
17. **piety** (pi-e-tee) n.	devoted in religion	The **devoted religious** people eat **pie** in church.
18. **hoodwink** (huud-wingk) v.	to deceive	The police were **deceived** when the **hoods winked**.
19. **curtail** (kur-tayl) v.	cut short, reduce	**Cut** the **tail short**.
20. **wry** (ri) adj.	twisted out of shape	The loaf of **rye** bread was **twisted.**

curs, curr—to run

The **runners** were **cursing** while they **ran.**

WORD ROOT	MEANING	ASSOCIATION
CURS, CURR	**to run**	The **runners** were **cursing** while they **ran**.
cursory (kur-sir-ee) adj.	hastily, hence often superficially, done.	
cursive (kur-siv) adj.	designating or of writing in which the letters are joined.	
currency (kur-en-see) n.	the money in circulation in any country.	
current (kur-ent) adj.	commonly accepted; in general use.	
curriculum (kur-rik-yoo-lum) n.	a course of study in school.	
currently (kur-ent-lee) adv.	now.	
MIGRA	**wander**	See tourists **wander** all around the top of **Miagra** Falls.
migrate (my-grayt) v.	leave to settle in another country or region.	
immigration (im-i-gray-shun) n.	the act of coming into a land.	
migratory (my-gra-tor-ee) adj.	wandering; as migratory birds.	
immigrate (im-i-grate) v.	to come into the land to settle.	
emigrate (em-i-grate) v.	to leave a land; to go out of a country.	
emigré (em-i-gray) n.	one forced to emigrate.	
TRA, TRANS	**across, through, over**	We'll take the **trains** all **through** and **across** Europe.
transportation (trans-por-tay-shun) n.	a means of conveyance.	
transplant (trans-plant) v.	to remove from one place and plant, resettle in another.	
transmit (trans-mit) v.	to send across to another person or place.	
transfer (trans-fur) v.	to carry, send to another person or place.	
transaction (trans-ak-shun) n.	performing or carrying out (business).	
traverse (tra-vurs) v.	to pass over, across, or through.	

REVIEW

Mark true or false in the space provided.

1. ______ To **abet** is to trick or deceive.
2. ______ A **nosegay** is one who is devoutly religious.
3. ______ To **mete** out is to distribute something.
4. ______ An **irony** is a deliberate insult.
5. ______ To **allay** is to bring calm to a situation.
6. ______ A **maverick** is a young animal.
7. ______ A **caret** is a book containing prayers.
8. ______ To **hoodwink** is to search thoroughly.
9. ______ A **wry** comment is one that is deliberately twisted.
10. ______ A **missal** is a small bouquet of flowers.

Mark the letter from column 2 that best describes each word in column 1.

1		2
curtail	______	a. to leave the country
affront	______	b. insult deliberately
ransack	______	c. to impose a tax
hamstring	______	d. to pass through
levy	______	e. religious
specter	______	f. to exchange remarks in a quarrel
fabricate	______	g. hastily done
bandy	______	h. to construct or invent
cursory	______	i. tendon behind the knee
gull	______	j. to cut short
emigrate	______	k. ghost
piety	______	l. to search thoroughly
traverse	______	m. to deceive

3

turnkey (turn-kee)—jailer

The **jailer turns** the **key** to lock the cell.

EXAMPLE OF USE

1. The **turnkey** announced that the prisoner had a visitor.

2. Alfred Hitchcock has received many **accolades** from his peers in the movie industry.

3. After such a hearty **repast**, I don't think I could eat any dessert.

4. "Shut your **maw**," said the farmer to the noisy cow.

5. The cave man hefted the **cudgel** up onto his shoulder and went hunting.

6. I prefer a good **claret** over all the other red wines.

7. In cold weather, a bowl of **pottage** can be very soothing.

8. The **coffers** of the kingdom were empty, so the king raised the taxes.

9. A bath is an **anathema** to most cats.

10. When the wine has been **decanted**, we'll be ready to make a toast.

11. I can't find this word in any **lexicon** in the library.

12. It is considered rude to **expectorate** in public.

13. The feminist movement has made it very unpopular to consider women as **chattel**.

14. He was at the **acme** of his career when illness forced him into early retirement.

15. What is that impressive looking **edifice**?

16. He has a **bovine** way of walking that makes me hope he never goes into a china shop.

17. "I'll consult with the **exchequer**," said the tourist, reaching for his wallet when approached by a beggar.

18. I appreciate a little **buffoonery** as a change of pace from my teacher's usual serious attitude.

19. I bought some bandaids at the local **apothecary**.

20. Now that we've been challenged, we must take up the **gauntlet** and meet our adversary fearlessly.

The most valuable of all talents is that of never using two words when one will do.
—Thomas Jefferson

	WORD	DEFINITION	ASSOCIATION
1.	**turnkey** (turn-kee) n.	jailer	The **jailer turns** the **key** to lock the cell.
2.	**accolade** (ak-o-layd) n.	honor, praise, approval	The **cool-aid** was given to **honor** and **praise** the students for good grades.
3.	**repast** (re-past) n.	meal	Hurry, it's way **past meal** time!
4.	**maw** (maw) n.	mouth or jaw of an animal	See the **mama** bear's big **jaw** and **mouth**!
5.	**cudgel** (kuj-el) n.	short, thick stick or club	See a person **cuddling** a big **club**.
6.	**claret** (klar-it) adj.	dark red color	The **clarinet** is painted a **deep red color**.
7.	**pottage** (pot-ij) n.	thick soup	The **pot's age** helps in cooking good **thick soup**.
8.	**coffer** (kaw-fer) n.	strongbox	See the **coffee** left in the **strong box**.
9.	**anathema** (a-nath-e-ma) n.	ban or curse, someone or thing detested	The national **anthem** was poorly sung and the fans **cursed**.
10.	**decant** (di-kant) v.	to pour from one container into another	See the "**Ds**" being **poured** from one **can** to another.
11.	**lexicon** (lek-si-kon) n.	dictionary of languages or branches of knowledge	**Leprechauns** only read the **dictionary**!
12.	**expectorate** (ik-spek-to-rayt) v.	to spit	I **expect** you won't **spit** in public!
13.	**chattel** (chat-el) n.	a moveable possession	The **cattle moved** their **possessions** into the barn.
14.	**acme** (ak-mee) n.	the highest point, peak of perfection	His **acne** was at its **peak** when he was at his **highest point** of perfection.
15.	**edifice** (ed-i-fis) n.	large building	**Ed**'s **office** is in a **large building**.
16.	**bovine** (boh-vine) adj.	of or like an ox or cow	See the **cows** and **oxen** wearing **bow-vines** (bow-ties?)
17.	**exchequer** (eks-chek-er) n.	a national treasury	Put your "**X**" on a **check** and mail it to the **national treasury**.
18.	**buffoon** (bu-foon) n.	clown, person who plays the fool	See the **clown** selling **balloons** (buffoons).
19.	**apothecary** (a-poth-e-ker-ee) n.	druggist	See the **pots carried** to the **druggist**.
20.	**gauntlet** (gawnt-lit) n.	medieval glove, punishment or blows from all sides at once	See your **Aunt letting** you have it with her **medieval glove**.

path—feeling, disease

The mountaineer **feels** his way along the **path**.

WORD ROOT	MEANING	ASSOCIATION
PATH	**feeling, disease**	The mountaineer **feels** his way along the **path**.
sympathy (sim-pa-thee) n.	sharing another person's emotions or feelings.	
telepathy (te-lep-e-thee) n.	communication of thoughts and feelings from one person to another over a distance.	
apathy (ap-a-thee) n.	lack of interest or emotional feelings.	
empathy (em-pa-thee) n.	the ability to identify oneself mentally with a person or thing and so understand his feelings.	
pathetic (pa-thet-ik) adj.	arousing feelings of pity or sadness.	
antipathy (an-tip-a-thee) n.	a strong feeling of dislike.	
TACT, TANG	**touch**	I **touched** the **tack** and it **stang**!
tact (takt) n.	the skillful touch of avoiding giving offense by saying or doing the right thing.	
tactile (tak-til) adj.	using the sense of touch.	
tactics (tak-tiks) n.	the art of placing or maneuvering forces skillfully in a battle.	
tangent (tan-jent) adj.	touching.	
intangible (in-tan-ji-bel) adj.	not touchable or material.	
contact (kon-takt) n.	touching, coming together.	
SENS, SENT	**feel, be aware**	The **incense** we **sent** will help you **feel** more **aware**.
sensitive (sen-si-tiv) adj.	alert and considerate about other people's feelings.	
sentiment (sen-ti-ment) n.	a mental attitude produced by one's feeling about something, an opinion.	
sense (sens) n.	ability to perceive or feel.	
sensual (sen-shoo-al) adj.	physical, gratifying feeling to the body and mind.	
sensation (sen-say-shon) n.	an awareness or feeling produced by stimulation of a sense organ or of the mind.	
consent (kon-sent) v.	to say that one is willing to do or allow what someone wishes.	

REVIEW

Mark the letter of the definition for each word in the space provided.

1. **maw**
   a. destruction b. animal's mouth c. gangster ______
2. **coffer**
   a. strongbox b. clown c. extreme fear ______
3. **gauntlet**
   a. punishment b. pardon c. jewel ______
4. **anathema**
   a. perfection b. a curse c. mournful song ______
5. **apothecary**
   a. druggist b. conversation c. agreement ______
6. **expectorate**
   a. to pour b. to destroy c. to spit ______
7. **pottage**
   a. building b. soup c. comment ______
8. **exchequer**
   a. national treasury b. dictionary c. pamphlet ______
9. **acme**
   a. cure b. perfection c. illusion ______
10. **cudgel**
    a. short stick b. possession c. kindness ______

Mark the letter or write the word that best completes each sentence.

1. The man who eyed the prisoner suspiciously is the ______.
   a. apothecary b. atrophy c. turnkey
2. A wine with a dark red color is a ______.
   a. gauntlet b. claret c. soliloquy
3. During the Middle Ages women and servants were treated as ______.
   a. chattel b. scuttle c. vagary
4. To understand a patient, the psychiatrist must have ______.
   a. antipathy b. arrogance c. empathy
5. The brightest person in class has received the most ______.
   a. abrogates b. accolades c. antedates
6. To enjoy sculpture, one should use the ______ sense.
   a. intangible b. viperous c. tactile
7. The loudest person telling a joke is often the ______.
   a. buffoon b. tankard c. wheedle
8. His father would not give ______ for him to go.
   a. verbose b. consent c. intrepid
9. She sat down at the table for the evening's ______.
   a. archives b. purloin c. repast
10. The answer to that question is not included in the ______.
    a. bigamy b. lexicon c. volition
11. The Empire State Building is no longer the largest ______.
    a. edifice b. olfactory c. raiment
12. The old woman is said to have a ______ disposition.
    a. vicarious b. tabloid c. bovine
13. It is best to ______ the wine before serving to bring out flavor.
    a. defecate b. decant c. decimate

garrulous (gar-ir-lus)—talkative
See a **gorrila talking** and yapping away.

EXAMPLE OF USE

1. The woman is **garrulous** because she's very lonely.

2. The name of Richard III has been **vilified** in story and song, despite the actual record of history.

3. Some Asians find our **occidental** point of view difficult to understand.

4. My professor is such a **cogent** speaker that I hesitate to disagree with him.

5. In springtime, kites are so **ubiquitous**, it's a wonder more of them don't get tangled up.

6. The angrier he got, the more **florid** his face became.

7. My plants, which have been **dormant** all winter, are suddenly blooming.

8. Some fairy tales are so **chimerical** that even young children know they couldn't be real.

9. The hills, which are normally brown, are **verdant**, thanks to the rainy winter.

10. The TV program is **didactic** to the point of dullness.

11. For Thanksgiving, we had **copious** servings of turkey and all the trimmings.

12. The events all seemed unrelated; it is difficult to understand how the detective could **concatenate** them all to solve the case.

13. I was **appalled** at the violence in that movie.

14. The **jocose** salesman had us all laughing so much that we bought the encyclopedia he was selling.

15. Just because the main character was **licentious** didn't mean the movie had to include such explicit sex scenes.

16. The professor's lectures tended to **obfuscate** rather than clarify.

17. Since I'm a **neophyte** at chess, please be patient with me.

18. I think your **pert** and impudent remarks call for an apology.

19. That comedian's act was too **risque** for our group.

20. The students showed their **reprobation** of his act by refusing to talk with him.

We should have a great many fewer disputes in the world if words were taken for what they are, signs of our ideas only, and not for things themselves.
—Locke, *Essay on the Human Understanding*

WORD	DEFINITION	ASSOCIATION
1. **garrulous** (gar-ir-lus) adj.	talkative	See a **gorilla talking** and yapping away.
2. **vilify** (vil-i-fi) n.	slander	Those **vile lies** about my **life** hurt me.
3. **occidental** (ok-si-den-tal) adj.	belonging to the West	It's no **accident** we live in the **West**.
4. **cogent** (koh-jent) adj.	convincing	The TV character **Kojak** is **forceful** and **convincing**.
5. **ubiquitous** (yoo-bik-wi-tus) adj.	occurring everywhere at same time	The kites **quit** on **us every where at the same time** the wind stopped.
6. **florid** (flor-id) adj.	rosy colored, ruddy	Buy your **rosy colored** roses at the **florist**.
7. **dormant** (dor-mant) adj.	sleeping, temporarily inactive	He is **asleep** on the **doormat**.
8. **chimerical** (ki-mer-i-kel) adj.	fantastic, wildly unreal	The **miracle** is **fantastic** and **wildly unreal**.
9. **verdant** (vur-dant) adj.	green with vegetation	Shall **vwe dance** in the lush **green vegetable** garden?
10. **didactic** (di-dak-tik) adj.	giving instruction	He **did act it** according to the **instructions** given.
11. **copious** (koh-pi-us) adj.	plentiful	The xerox machine makes **plenty** of **copies**.
12. **concatenation** (kon-kat-e-nay-shon) n.	active linking of ideas, facts together	See the **con's cat nation actively chained together**.
13. **appall** (a-pawl) v.	to fill with horror, shock	**A pole** was electrified, **shocked** and **filled** him **with horror**.
14. **jocose** (joh-kohs) adj.	joking	**Joke** sounds like **jocose**.
15. **licentious** (li-sen-shus) adj.	immoral, lewd	You need a **license** to act **immoral** and **lewd**.
16. **obfuscate** (ob-fus-kayt) v.	to darken, obscure, confuse, muddy	**If you skate** through **mud**, you'll **darken** 'em.
17. **neophyte** (nee-o-fite) n.	beginner, novice	A **new fighter** enters the ring like a **beginner**.
18. **pert** (purt) adj.	bold	Would I be **bold** to say you're **perty**?
19. **risque** (ri-skay) adj.	of questionable decency; naughty; off-color	Don't **risk** your reputation with **naughty**, **off-color** remarks.
20. **reprobate** (re-ro-bayt) adj.	villain, immoral person	The **villain** is on **probation**.

cardi—heart

See the **heart** on the **cards**.

WORD ROOT	MEANING	ASSOCIATION
CARDI	**heart**	The **heart** is on the **cards**.
cardiac (kahr-di-ak) adj.	of the heart.	
cardiologist (kahr-di-ol-o-jist) n.	specialist in cardiology.	
cardiology (kahr-di-ol-o-jee) n.	branch of medicine dealing with the heart, its movement, function, diseases.	
cardiopulmonary (kahr-di-oh-pul-mu-ner-ee) adj.	of or involving heart and lungs.	
electrocardiograph (i-lect-troh-kahr-di-o-graf) n.	a device that detects and records electric activity in muscles of the heart.	
cardiovascular (kahr-di-oh-vas-kyu-lar) adj.	of or involving the blood vessels and heart.	
HEMA, HEMO	**blood**	**Hey ma!**, **hey mo!**, there's **blood**!
hemophilia (hee-mo-fil-i-a) n.	inherited tendency to bleed severely from even a slight cut.	
hemachrome (hee-ma-krome) n.	the red pigment of the blood.	
hematoxic (hee-mo-tok-sik) adj.	causing blood poisoning.	
hemorrhage (hem-o-rij) n.	bleeding extensively.	
hemoglobin (hee-mo-gloh-bin) n.	red oxygen carrying substance in blood.	
hemostat (hee-mo-stat) n.	chemical agent or device used to reduce or stop bleeding during surgery.	
BIO	**life**	**By-o** the way, how's **life**?
biology (by-ol-o-jee) n.	scientific study of life and living things.	
biography (by-og-ra-fee) n.	person's life story written by someone else.	
biostatistics (by-o-sta-tis-tiks) n.	statistics relating to life.	
biopsy (by-op-see) n.	examination of tissue from living body.	
autobiography (aw-toh-by-og-ra-fee) n.	life story written by that person.	
biognosis (by-og-no-sis) n.	the inquiry into or the study of life.	

REVIEW

Draw a line between the word and its correct definition.

1. **vilify**	a. immoral
2. **licentious**	b. green with vegetation
3. **hemorrhage**	c. rosy colored
4. **dormant**	d. occurring everywhere
5. **risque**	e. bold
6. **cardiopulmonary**	f. examination of human tissue
7. **occidental**	g. convincing
8. **florid**	h. slander
9. **biopsy**	i. belonging to the West
10. **verdant**	j. involving the heart and lungs
11. **ubiquitous**	k. sleeping
12. **cogent**	l. naughty
13. **pert**	m. extensive bleeding

Circle the correct word below each definition.

1. **unreal**
   (ubiquitous, benevolent, chimerical, contiguous)
2. **to fill with horror**
   (reprobate, perambulate, appall, assimilate)
3. **plentiful**
   (copious, jocose, transient, congruous)
4. **talkative**
   (parsimonious, garrulous, itinerant, gourmand)
5. **beginner**
   (neophyte, ectomorph, obloquy, necropsy)
6. **to confuse**
   (rebuff, obfuscate, harangue, obviate)
7. **linking facts together**
   (ornithology, concatenation, libation, calumniation)
8. **giving instructions**
   (didactic, arable, tenuous, diatribe)
9. **joking**
   (fetid, laudatory, jocose, jargon)
10. **immoral person**
    (misnomer, reprobate, arabesque, reveller)

effete (i-feet)—worn out, exhausted

See the **feet** are **worn out** and **exhausted.**

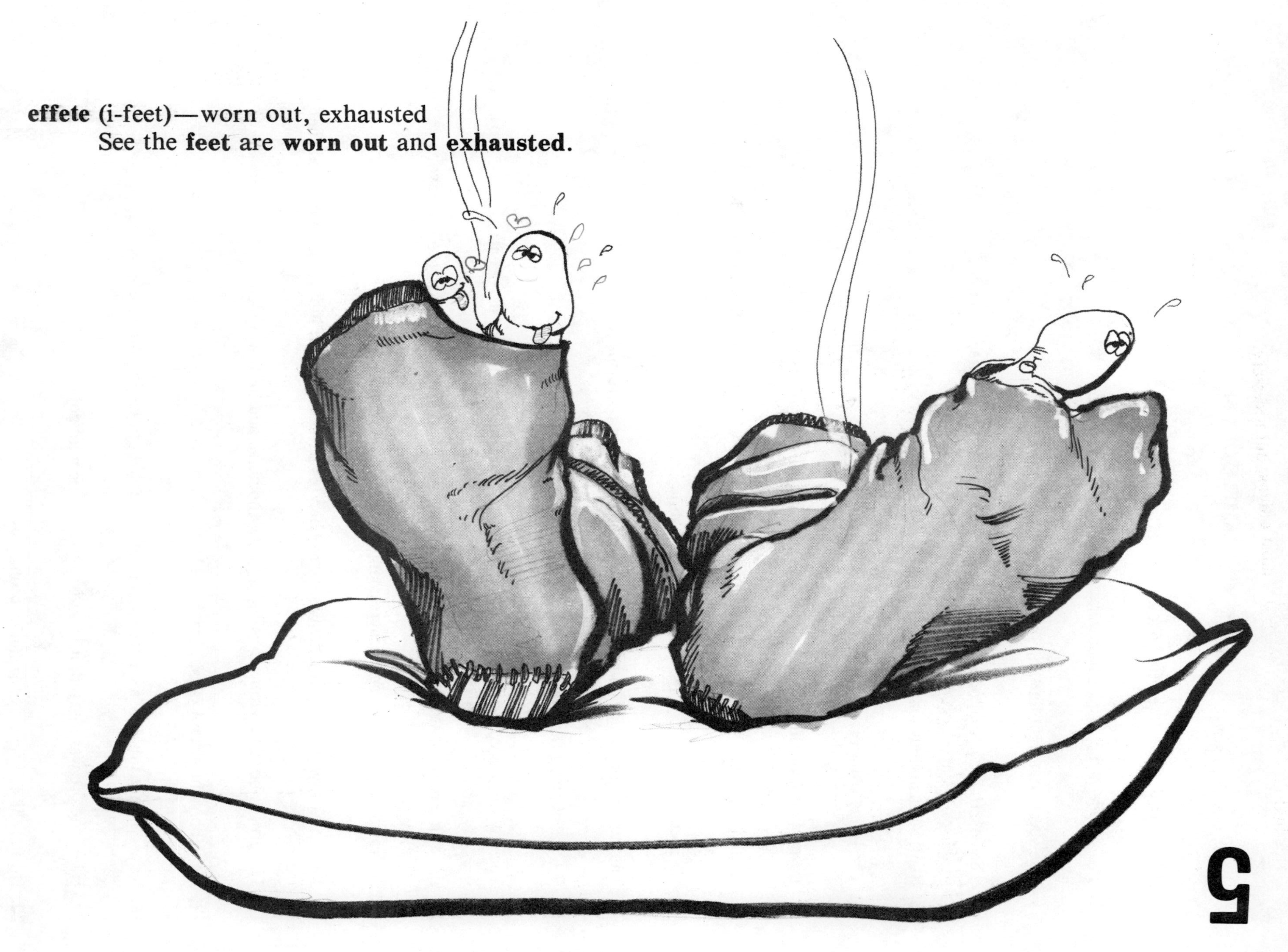

EXAMPLE OF USE

1. After the war, our literature showed the **effete** condition of the writers who had lived through it.

2. It **disconcerts** me to hear that there are going to be layoffs.

3. The speedboat went **hurtling** over the waves.

4. The coach attempted to **goad** his team to victory with an inspired pep talk.

5. She's so **fastidious** that she won't drink from anyone else's glass, even if she's dying of thirst.

6. The judge's stern **visage** indicated that his verdict would be "guilty."

7. If you **juxtapose** the two photos, you'll see that the color doesn't match.

8. Congress keeps farm prices at 80 percent **parity** with prices of manufactured goods.

9. He is **enamored** of the star of that new TV show.

10. The supervisor **castigated** his department for their poor performance.

11. We sailed along the **fjords** on our trip to Norway.

12. The lawyer delivered a **tirade** to the jury in order to win the case for his client.

13. It's a rare head of state who doesn't encounter **sycophants**, always looking to win favor.

14. Although we have had our disagreements, I bear you no **animosity**.

15. The priest saw the baby for the first time when his parents brought him to the baptismal **font**.

16. The groom became **wroth** when he saw how the horse had been whipped.

17. He dabbles in **metaphysics**, because he loves to ponder the nature of the universe.

18. Now he claims that he's innocent, that he made that confession under **duress**.

19. When the ore was **assayed**, it was discovered to be pure gold.

20. During the eclipse only the sun's **corona** was visible.

WORD	DEFINITION	ASSOCIATION
1. **effete** (i-feet) adj.	worn out, exhausted	See the **feet** are **worn out** and **exhausted.**
2. **disconcert** (dis-kon-surt) v.	to disturb; fluster	This **concert disturbs** me.
3. **hurtle** (hur-tel) v.	to speed	That **hurtler** possesses amazing **speed!**
4. **goad** (gohd) v.	to spur	See the **goat** jump when hit by the **spurs.**
5. **fastidious** (fa-stid-i-us) adj.	choosing only what is good	**Fast** and **tidy** people **choose only what's good.**
6. **visage** (viz-ij) n.	face; appearance	His **visible age** showed in his **face** and **appearance.**
7. **juxtapose** (juk-sta-pohz) v.	place side by side	**Just pose** before the camera **side by side.**
8. **parity** (par-i-tee) n.	equality	My **party** is **equally** as good today as yesterday.
9. **enamored** (i-nam-ord) adj.	be inspired to love	**Amour** means **love.**
10. **castigate** (kas-ti-gayt) v.	punish by blows; criticize severely	Don't **punish** someone by **casting** them into **a gate.**
11. **fjord** (fyohrd) n.	long, narrow inlet from sea	See a **Ford** floating into the **sea's long narrow inlets.**
12. **tirade** (ti-rayd) n.	long, vehement speech	I'm **tired** of **long vehement speeches** from dad.
13. **sycophant** (sik-o-fant) n.	flatterer, parasite	See the **sick elephant flatten** a **pear on site.**
14. **animosity** (an-i-mos-i-tee) n.	hatred, hostility	**Animal haters** are **hostile** people.
15. **font** (font) n.	church basin; set of printing type of one style & size	He is **printing type** in **front** of the **church basin.**
16. **wroth** (rawth) adj.	old use—angry; new use—wrath	**Wroth** and **wrath** sound alike.
17. **metaphysics** (met-a-fiz-iks) n.	philosophy dealing with nature of existence	I **met** a **physics** teacher whose **philosophy** was "the **nature of existence.**"
18. **duress** (duu-res) n.	use of force or threats to procure something	Do I have to **threaten** and **force** the children to get **dressed?**
19. **assay** (as-ay) n.	analyze chemically to test for composition & quality	The **essay** will contain my **chemical analysis.**
20. **corona** (ko-roh-na) n.	crown, luminous circle	The **crown** of the **sun's light** shines brilliantly.

graph—write, record, draw, describe

Write, describe and **draw** a **record** on **graph** paper.

WORD ROOT	MEANING	ASSOCIATION
GRAPH	**write, record, draw, describe**	**Write, describe** and **draw** a **record** on **graph** paper.
graph (graf) n.	a diagram representing the successive changes in the value of a variable quantity.	
geography (jee-og-ra-fe) n.	scientific recorded study of Earth's surface and features.	
lexicographer (lek-si-kog-ra-fur) n.	one who compiles a dictionary.	
calligraphy (ka-lig-ra-fee) n.	beautiful handwriting.	
graphology (gra-fol-o-jee) n.	scientific study of handwriting especially as a guide to writer's character.	
photograph (foh-to-graf) n.	picture formed by means of the chemical action of light on a light-sensitive surface.	
PICT, PICTO	**paint**	**Pick two paint** brushes for the job.
picture (pik-chur) n.	resemblance of a person, place or thing made by painting, etc., especially as a work of art.	
pictograph (pik-to-graf) n.	a pictorial symbol.	
picturesque (pik-chu-resk) adj.	forming a striking and pleasant scene.	
pictorial (pik-tor-i-al) adj.	of or expressed in a picture or pictures.	
pictury (pik-tur-ee) adj.	tending to look like a picture.	
depict (de-pikt) v.	to show in the form of a picture or describe in words.	
TELE	**far, distant**	A **telescope** sees **far** into the **distance**!
telegraphy (te-leg-ra-fee) n.	process of communication by telegraph.	
telephone (tel-e-fohn) n.	system of transmitting sound over distance.	
telephotograph (tel-e-foh-to-graf) n.	photograph of a distant object by combination telescope and ordinary photographic lens.	
telecast (tel-e-kast) v.	to broadcast by television from a distance.	
televise (tel-e-viz) v.	to transmit by television from a distance.	
teletypewriter (tel-e-tiep-ri-ter) n.	a telegraph instrument for transmitting messages by typing.	

REVIEW

Mark true or false in the space provided.

1. ________ A **font** is a set of printing type.
2. ________ To go on a **tirade** is to leave the ground.
3. ________ To be **fastidious** is to be in love.
4. ________ A **fjord** is a narrow inlet from the sea.
5. ________ **Animosity** is a form of kindness to animals.
6. ________ To achieve **parity** means to be equal.
7. ________ A **corona** is a luminous circle.
8. ________ **Metaphysics** is the study of muscle development.
9. ________ A **sycophant** is someone who dances to swing music.
10. ________ To **disconcert** is to disturb another person.

Mark the letter from column 2 that best describes each word in column 1.

1		2
effete	________	a. appearance
wroth	________	b. criticize severely
calligraphy	________	c. place side by side
enamored	________	d. to spur
picturesque	________	e. to broadcast by television
goad	________	f. use of force to procure something
hurtle	________	g. inspired by love
duress	________	h. worn out
assay	________	i. a pleasant scene
telecast	________	j. wrath
visage	________	k. to analyze chemically
juxtapose	________	l. to speed
castigate	________	m. the art of handwriting

sojourn (soh-jurn)—to stay at a place temporarily
"**So journey** no more, **stay awhile.**"

EXAMPLE OF USE

1. I have come from the East Coast to **sojourn** in California for a while.
2. That dictionary is the largest **tome** in the library.
3. His conduct during the funeral ceremony was **staid** and solemn.
4. I do not **relish** the idea of staying late after school.
5. The chemist had concocted a mysterious drug, which he kept in a **phial.**
6. That little man looks just like a **gnome** in a fairy tale.
7. Before pronouncing sentence, the judge read a short **homily** to the criminal.
8. It must be **kismet** that brought us together.
9. She was **inundated** with gifts when she announced her engagement.
10. It would take a lot to get her excited, since she's so **jaded.**
11. It would be a **misnomer** to call her a lady.
12. The girl's **winsome** face had attracted many admirers.
13. She appeared calm and **placid,** although she was really very upset.
14. This bank will **vouchsafe** a loan only if your credit is exceptionally good.
15. He was at the **zenith** of his career when he decided to marry.
16. This decision is bound to **foment** disagreement among the union members.
17. After severe **holocausts** like floods and fires, architects learn to design more substantial buildings.
18. The **saline** content of that water makes it unsafe for drinking.
19. After mowing the lawn, he was glad to lie **supine** in the hammock.
20. He was so angry that his face became **livid.**

Size of vocabulary and number of ideas are intimately related. A mastery of a large number of words . . . can lead to a greater range of thought. —Joseph G. Brin

WORD	DEFINITION	ASSOCIATION *Where examples are not given, create and write your associations in the spaces provided!*
1. **sojourn** (soh-jurn) v.	to stay at a place temporarily	**So journey** no more, **stay awhile.**
2. **tome** (tohm) n.	large volume	The tome (tomb) answered many question the volume presented
3. **staid** (stayd) adj.	sober, serious, sedate	The drunk said "I wished I'd **staid sober**"—hic.
4. **relish** (rel-ish) n.	savor, enjoy	Do you enjoy/relish on your hamburger?
5. **phial** (fi-al) n.	small bottle, a vial	See the **small bottle** in the **file** cabinet.
6. **gnome** (nohm) n.	dwarf	dome is like Giant Gnome is a dwarf
7. **homily** (hom-i-lee) n.	sermon	Why do I only get **sermons** when I'm **home**?
8. **kismet** (kiz-mit) n.	fate	We kiss when we met just like it was fate.
9. **inundate** (in-un-dayt) v.	overflow, to flood	**On** the **date** the compliments were **overflowing**.
10. **jaded** (jay-did) adj.	fatigue, boredom	Jay did look bored he'll never figure out the surprise
11. **misnomer** (mis-noh-mer) n.	wrong name applied to something	I **missed** the **name** and introduced him **incorrectly**.
12. **winsome** (win-som) adj.	agreeable, gracious manner	She always a winssome because everyone likes her agreeable gracious manner
13. **placid** (plas-id) adj.	peaceful, calm	Lake **Placid** was **calm** after the storm.
14. **vouchsafe** (vowch-saff) v.	to permit	I vouched safely for your early permit
15. **zenith** (zee-nith) n.	highest point	Let's watch the lodge's **Zenith** TV at the **peak**.
16. **foment** (foh-ment) v.	stir up, stimulate, arouse	Foment to solve prob, not arouse them.
17. **holocaust** (hol-o-kowst) n.	destruction by fire	See the **fire** burned the **hollow** of the tree.
18. **saline** (say-leen) adj.	salty	to stay lean don't use to much salt
19. **supine** (soo-pine) adj.	lying on the back; not inclined to take action	See the **pine** tree **lying** on its **back**.
20. **livid** (liv-id) adj.	enraged; color of black and blue	He livid in a black and blue house

super—over, above, greater in quality

Superman flies **above** and **over** the city.

WORD ROOT	MEANING	ASSOCIATION *Where examples are not given, create and write your associations in the spaces provided!*
SUPER	**over, above, greater in quality**	**Superman** flies **above** and **over** the city.
superhuman (soo-per-hyoo-man) adj.	beyond ordinary human capacity.	
superfine (soo-per-fyn) adj.	high quality.	
superable (soo-pe-ra-bl) adj.	can be overcome, conquered, or surmounted.	
supercilious (soo-per-sil-i-us) adj.	with an air of superiority.	
superiority (soo-peer-i-or-i-tee) n.	higher in quality, position or rank.	
superimpose (soo-per-im-pohz) v.	to lay or place one thing on top of another.	
FORC, FORT	**strong**	He used his strength to force the kid in his car
force (fohrs) n.	strength, power, intense effort	
enforce (en-fohrs) v.	to impose by force or compulsion.	
effortless (ef-ort-lis) adj.	done without strenuous effort.	
fortitude (for-ti-tood) n.	strength and courage in time of trouble.	
comfortable (kumf-ta-bel) adj.	not close or restricted.	
fortissimo (for-tis-i-moh) adv.	very strong and loud, especially in music.	
SUB	**under, beneath**	The nuclear **sub** patrols **underwater** year-round.
subject (sub-jekt) v.	to bring under one's control.	
subconscious (sub-kon-shus) n.	part of mind beneath conscious mind.	
subdue (sub-doo) v.	to bring under control.	
submission (sub-mish-on) n.	act of surrender to authority.	
subterfuge (sub-ter-fyooj) n.	excuse used to avoid blame.	
subversive (sub-ver-siv) adj.	attempting to overthrow authority by weakening people's trust or belief.	

REVIEW

Mark the letter of the correct word for each definition in the space provided.

1. **to arouse** ______
   a. foment b. purge c. attest
2. **sermon** ______
   a. nemesis b. homily c. quorum
3. **peaceful** ______
   a. bedlam b. placid c. succulent
4. **fate** ______
   a. necrophobia b. kismet c. osteopathy
5. **enraged** ______
   a. asinine b. beatific c. livid
6. **dwarf** ______
   a. avoirdupois b. pseudonym c. gnome
7. **small bottle** ______
   a. tome b. phial c. kudos
8. **wrong name** ______
   a. bibliophile b. usury c. misnomer
9. **salty** ______
   a. saturnine b. onerous c. saline
10. **serious** ______
    a. staid b. pithy c. raucous

Mark the letter or write the word that best completes each sentence.

1. The paramedics at the scene responded with ______.
   a. regatta b. fortitude c. pyrophobia
2. While in Europe, the professor decided to ______ in Venice.
   a. opuscle b. truncheon c. sojourn
3. An unabridged dictionary would be a lengthy ______.
   a. tome b. vogue c. hybrid
4. Jim is at the ______ of his career.
   a. prig b. zenith c. affluence
5. The ballerina was resting in a ______ position.
   a. supine b. benign c. salutary
6. The students were ______ with work.
   a. stilted b. inundated c. beseeched
7. The graduate student looked at the dunce with a ______ grin.
   a. superficial b. supercilious c. fledgling
8. The young bride has a ______ manner.
   a. winsome b. effete c. infernal
9. The baseball players jumped into the game with ______.
   a. guffaw b. relish c. junket
10. Older people tend to be more ______ about life than children.
    a. jaded b. vivacious c. frenetic
11. Third World governments are often subject to ______ plots.
    a. submissive b. subversive c. herbivorous
12. The president would not ______ additional criticism from his staff.
    a. vouchsafe b. commiserate c. decapitate
13. Arson was suspected in the ______ at the hotel.
    a. hyperbole b. holocaust c. agglutination

rabid (rab-id)—fanatical, furious
Ever see an **angry, furious rabbit** before?

EXAMPLE OF USE

1. If you are bitten by a squirrel, check with the doctor because the animal may be **rabid**.
2. Bullets flew **pell-mell,** and we all ducked.
3. He was deep in the **throes** of his first love affair.
4. He's such a **glib** talker that only later are you apt to question his credibility.
5. He **mused** on the ironic nature of life.
6. He **enthralls** audiences with his fine song-and-dance routine.
7. He was so **hirsute** that even when he became bald, he had more hair than the average man.
8. When the air conditioner broke, we **sweltered** until it was fixed.
9. One of the basic **tenets** of a democracy is the right to vote.
10. She has an **uncanny** way of knowing what is going to happen before it actually happens.
11. To **whet** your appetite, let me tell you what we're having for dinner.
12. His behavior was so **obnoxious,** he was asked to leave the party.
13. He began to **prattle** in order to cover up his nervousness.
14. The congressman said it was a fact-finding trip, but it turned out to be just another **junket**.
15. He **vented** his emotions by hitting the wall.
16. Some desert tribes are **nomadic** and live in tents.
17. "Have a nice trip," he **quipped** when she tripped on a banana peel.
18. He feared the dangers of the world, so he became a **recluse**.
19. I tried to **wrest** the sharp toy away from the baby's grasp.
20. He was a pacifist and did not wish to enter the **fray**.

The limits of my language stand for the limits of my world.
—Ludwig Wittgenstein

WORD	DEFINITION	ASSOCIATION *Where examples are not given, create and write your associations in the spaces provided!*
1. **rabid** (rab-id) adj.	fanatical, furious	Ever see an **angry, furious rabbit** before?
2. **pell-mell** (pel-mel) adj.	in confused haste, disorder	
3. **throes** (throhs) n.	a severe pang of pain, violent anguish	When **thrown** down, I felt a **sharp pain.**
4. **glib** (glib) adj.	smooth, slippery, fluent	
5. **muse** (my-oz) v.	to ponder	Let's sit in the **pond** and enjoy the **music.**
6. **enthrall** (en-thrawl) v.	hold spellbound, capture, make slave	
7. **hirsute** (hur-soot) adj.	hairy	**Her suit** is very **hairy.**
8. **swelter** (swel-ter) v.	suffer from heat	
9. **tenet** (ten-it) n.	doctrine	Into the **tent** the **doctor** went.
10. **uncanny** (un-kan-ee) adj.	strange, mysterious	
11. **whet** (hwet) v.	sharpen, stimulate	**Whet** the **sharpening** stone.
12. **obnoxious** (ob-nok-shis) adj.	offensive	
13. **prattle** (prat-el) n.	childish chatter	Stop your **childish tattling.**
14. **junket** (jung-kit) n.	a trip taken at public expense	
15. **vent** (vent) v.	express freely	This **express vent** releases excess air.
16. **nomadic** (nah-mad-ik) adj.	wandering	
17. **quip** (kwip) n.	witty or sarcastic comment	**Quip** (quit) making those **sarcastic remarks.**
18. **recluse** (ri-klous) n.	hermit	
19. **wrest** (rest) v.	pull away	I **wrestled away** from him when he grabbed me.
20. **fray** (fray) n.	a fight	

extra—outside

Outside, the paper heralds **Extra, Extra**!

WORD ROOT	MEANING	ASSOCIATION *Where examples are not given, create and write your associations in the spaces provided!*
EXTRA	**outside**	**Outside**, the paper heralds **Extra, Extra!**
extraordinary (ik-stror-di-ner-ee) adj.	very unusual or remarkable.	
extraterrestrial (ek-stra-te-res-tri-al) adj.	of or from outside Earth or its atmosphere.	
extraneous (ik-stray-ni-us) adj.	not belonging to the matter or subject in hand.	
extramarital (ek-stra-mar-i-tal) adj.	sexual relationships outside marriage.	
extracurricular (ek-stra-ku-rik-yu-lar) adj.	not within curriculum, sports.	
extradite (ek-stra-diyt) v.	to hand over (a person accused or convicted of a crime) to the country where crime was committed.	
AB	**away from, separation**	________________________
abnormal (ab-norm-al) adj.	different from what is normal.	
abstract (ab-strakt) v.	to take out; separate.	
absorb (ab-sorb) v.	to take in; combine.	
absolve (ab-zolv) v.	to clear of blame or guilt.	
abrogate (ab-ro-gayt) v.	to cancel; to take away.	
abjure (ab-joor) v.	to renounce under oath.	
RE	**back, again**	**Re-set** your watch, daylight savings is **back again**.
recall (ri-kawl) v.	to summon a person to return; bring back to mind.	
remarry (ri-ma-ree) v.	to wed again.	
repeat (ri-peet) v.	to say or do or occur again.	
repay (ri-pay) v..	to pay back.	
rewrite (ree-rit) v.	to write again in a different form.	
reiterate (re-it-e-rayt) v.	to say or do again.	

REVIEW

Draw a line between the word and its correct definition.

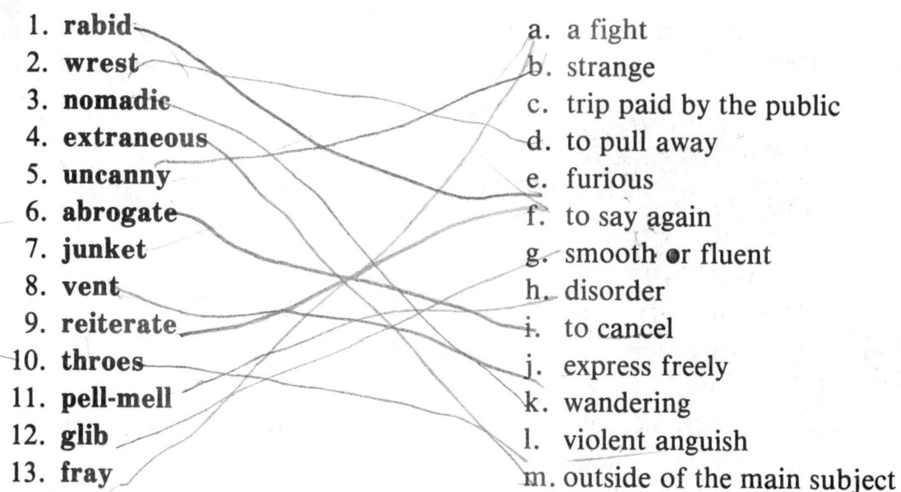

1. **rabid**	a. a fight
2. **wrest**	b. strange
3. **nomadic**	c. trip paid by the public
4. **extraneous**	d. to pull away
5. **uncanny**	e. furious
6. **abrogate**	f. to say again
7. **junket**	g. smooth or fluent
8. **vent**	h. disorder
9. **reiterate**	i. to cancel
10. **throes**	j. express freely
11. **pell-mell**	k. wandering
12. **glib**	l. violent anguish
13. **fray**	m. outside of the main subject

Circle the correct word below each definition.

1. **doctrine**
   (anomaly, tenet, anagram, autonomy)
2. **stimulate**
   (whet, berate, malign, abhor)
3. **hairy**
   (sanguine, pallid, hirsute, repulsive)
4. **to suffer from heat**
   (putrefy, vacillate, swelter, surrogate)
5. **witty comment**
   (disparity, eulogy, quip, aplomb)
6. **to ponder**
   (capitulate, muse, mollify, personify)
7. **offensive**
   (erudite, scrupulous, obnoxious, explicit)
8. **childish chatter**
   (curriculum, epithet, prattle, cheroot)
9. **hermit**
   (recluse, philanderer, raconteur, pugilist)
10. **to hold spellbound**
    (intimidate, induce, enthrall, interpolate)

sonorous (so-nohr-us)—resonant, giving a deep, powerful sound
See a man **sonoring loudly**.

EXAMPLE OF USE

1. His **sonorous** voice resounded through the auditorium.
2. If we can estimate how much of the land is **arable**, we can project how much food we can grow.
3. It would be hard to dance to that song; it's like a **dirge**.
4. If you stray from the terms of our **covenant**, I can take you to court.
5. The cat **disported** itself by attacking a toy mouse.
6. It may not be an ideal solution, but it's a **pragmatic** one.
7. The edict met with such protest that the mayor **rescinded** it.
8. After the accident he decided to **scuttle** the boat, rather than tow it back to shore and repair it.
9. Let's be on the **qui vive**, in case he tries to surprise us.
10. The **pathos** in his story touched me deeply.
11. I've entered my sloop in the **regatta**; with a good crew she might win.
12. He is such an **obdurate** person, so set in his opinions, that no one can reason with him.
13. My dog may be **puny**, but he's surprisingly tough.
14. He's very **taciturn**, and it often makes me wonder what he's thinking.
15. Penicillin can cure many diseases, but it's not a **panacea**.
16. The **noxious** fumes from the solvent are hurting my eyes.
17. Before the exam, I will **iterate** one last time the main points to be covered.
18. **Ribald** stories are okay with me, but I know my mother disapproves of them.
19. The **inveterate** bachelor is wary of marriage.
20. He used a well-known **ruse** to get her to turn around.

WORD	DEFINITION	ASSOCIATION *Where examples are not given, create and write your associations in the spaces provided!*
1. **sonorous** (so-nohr-us) adj.	resonant, giving a deep powerful sound	See a man **sonoring loudly**.
2. **arable** (ar-a-bel) adj.	fit for plowing	____________________
3. **dirge** (durj) n.	slow, mournful song	**He'd urged** us to listen to that **slow, sad song**.
4. **covenant** (kuv-e-nant) n.	formal agreement	____________________
5. **disport** (di-sporht) v.	amuse oneself, play	**This sport** is quite **amusing**.
6. **pragmatic** (prag-mat-ik) adj.	practical viewpoint	____________________
7. **rescind** (ri-sind) v.	cancel	**Re send** us the **cancelled** order.
8. **scuttle** (skut-el) v.	sink a ship	____________________
9. **qui vive** (kee-veev) French adj.	alert, watchful	The night watchman was **alert, keys in view**.
10. **pathos** (pay-thos) n.	quality that arouses pity, compassion	____________________
11. **regatta** (ri-gat-a) n.	boat or yacht race	"**We gotto** leave for the **boat race**."
12. **obdurate** (ob-du-rit) adj.	stubborn and unyielding	____________________
13. **puny** (pyoo-nee) adj.	tiny, undersized, weak	See the **pony undersized** and **weak**.
14. **taciturn** (tas-i-turn) adj.	habitually silent, talking little	____________________
15. **panacea** (pan-a-see-a) n.	cure-all	**Pancakes** for breakfast are a **cure-all**.
16. **noxious** (nok-shus) adj.	harmful, unpleasant	____________________
17. **iterate** (it-e-rayt) v.	repeat	It's **irritating** when someone **repeats** himself!
18. **ribald** (rib-ald) adj.	vulgar humor	____________________
19. **inveterate** (in-vet-e-rit) adj.	confirmed, habitual	See the **veteran confirmed** in his beliefs against war.
20. **ruse** (rooz) n.	trick	____________________

contr, contra—against

He bumped **against** the restaurant **counter**.

WORD ROOT	MEANING	ASSOCIATION *Where examples are not given, create and write your associations in the spaces provided!*
CONTR, CONTRA	**against**	He bumped **against** the restaurant **counter**.
contrast (kon-trast) n.	a striking difference between things being compared.	
contradiction (kon-tra-dik-shun) n.	to assert the opposite of.	
contradistinction (kon-tra-dis-tink-shun) n.	distinction by opposite qualities or contrast.	
contrary (kon-trer-ee) adj.	opposed, altogether different.	
contrapuntally (kon-tra-pun-tul-ee) adv.	in a manner conforming to the rules of counterpoint.	
contrariwise (kon-trer-ee-wize) adv.	in the opposite way or order.	
ANTI, ANT	**against**	~~It was the ants vs. our~~ lunch! the ants won!
antithesis (an-tith-e-sis) n.	the exact opposite.	
antifreeze (an-ti-freez) n.	a substance used to prevent freezing.	
antidote (an-ti-doht) n.	a remedy to counteract a poison.	
anticlimax (an-ti-kli-maks) n.	a sudden drop from the important to the unimportant.	
antipodes (an-tip-e-dez) n.	two places directly opposite each other on the Earth.	
antagonism (an-tag-o-niz-em) v.	the state of being in active opposition; hostility against.	
DIS	**take away, not**	**Take away dis** car, it's **not** supposed to be here.
disapprove (dis-e-proov) v.	to not approve.	
discourage (dis-kur-ij) v.	to persuade (a person) to refrain.	
disease (di-zeez) n.	illness in general.	
disaster (di-zas-ter) n.	any happening that causes great harm or damage.	
dispose (di-spohz) v.	to place suitably or in order.	
disinherit (dis-in-her-it) v.	to deprive of an inheritance.	

REVIEW

Mark true or false in the space provided.

1. ______ **Pathos** involves one's sense of pity.
2. ______ A **ruse** is a form of vegetable.
3. ______ To **disport** is to stop the game.
4. ______ A **regatta** is a boat race.
5. ______ **Panacea** is another word for the stomach.
6. ______ **Arable** land is fit for plowing.
7. ______ **Qui vive** is a type of French cooking.
8. ______ To **scuttle** a ship is to cause it to sink.
9. ______ A **pragmatic** approach to life is to be wild and free.
10. ______ A **dirge** is a type of boat used on rivers.

Mark the letter from column 2 that best describes each word in column 1.

1		2
contradistinction	______	a. formal agreement
inveterate	______	b. deep, powerful sound
covenant	______	c. harmful
sonorous	______	d. habitually silent
rescind	______	e. opposite qualities
antithesis	______	f. vulgar humor
obdurate	______	g. habitual
noxious	______	h. to cancel
ribald	______	i. to leave out of the will
puny	______	j. to repeat
disinherit	______	k. stubborn
iterate	______	l. undersized
taciturn	______	m. the exact opposite

quandary (kwon-da-ree)—state of perplexity, dilemma
The housewife is in a **dilemma** over the **laundary**!

EXAMPLE OF USE

1. I am in a **quandary** as to which dessert to choose.

2. Despite his **blandishments**, she rejected his offer to take her out to dinner.

3. He worked at a **frenetic** pace until the job was done.

4. He uses a lot of clichés, which make his speeches very **banal**.

5. Social workers hope to **ameliorate** the conditions of the poor.

6. As we examine the **dialectic** of these two viewpoints, let's see if there is any way their positions can be reconciled.

7. The toothless **crone** frightened us when she laughed.

8. I enjoyed our **colloquy**, even though we didn't really come to any conclusions.

9. Daniel Boone was an **intrepid** frontiersman.

10. After the **poignant** movie, I left the theater with tears still on my cheeks.

11. The **motif** of birds recurs in each of his paintings.

12. In the story of *Moby Dick*, the whale is Captain Ahab's **nemesis**.

13. He gave a mighty **guffaw** when the comedian told a funny story.

14. The **homogeneous** student body will change when the school is integrated.

15. The professor was so **erudite**, it was difficult to have an ordinary conversation with him.

16. These pills are to be taken **diurnally** in order for them to be effective.

17. The **crux** of the problem seems to be that we are using the same word to mean different things.

18. Because his praise was so **fulsome**, she suspected he had ulterior motives.

19. He is popular because of his **benign** attitude toward both friends and strangers.

20. He didn't want to be **encumbered** while traveling, so he only carried a knapsack.

We have too many high sounding words, and too few actions that correspond with them.
—Abigail Adams

WORD	DEFINITION	ASSOCIATION *Where examples are not given, create and write your associations in the spaces provided!*
1. **quandary** (kwon-da-ree) n.	state of perplexity, dilemma	The housewife is in a **dilemma** over the **laundary**!
2. **blandishment** (blan-dish-ment) n.	flattering speech or action	He flattered the dish that was not ment to be bland
3. **frenetic** (fre-net-ik) adj.	frantic	**Frenetic** sounds like **frantic**.
4. **banal** (ba-nal) adj.	commonplace	
5. **ameliorate** (a-meel-yo-rate) v.	improve, make better	He **improved** in **Amelia's rating**.
6. **dialectic** (di-a-lek-tik) n.	art of debating, systematic reasoning	
7. **crone** (krohn) n.	hag, withered old woman	There was a **crown** on the ugly **hag's** head.
8. **colloquy** (kol-o-kwee) n.	a conversation	
9. **intrepid** (in-trep-id) adj.	fearless	Even when **entrapped**, he was **fearless**.
10. **poignant** (poin-yant) adj.	keenly felt	keenly felt
11. **motif** (moh-teef) n.	theme	The **motive** is the **theme** of the story.
12. **nemesis** (nem-e-sis) n.	revenging agent	
13. **guffaw** (gu-faw) n.	coarse loud laughter	Picture the **goof-off laughing loudly**.
14. **homogeneous** (hoh-mo-jee-ni-us) adj.	of same kind	
15. **erudite** (er-yu-dit) adj.	scholarly, learned	A scholar often has **a rude attitude**.
16. **diurnal** (di-ur-nal) adj.	daily	
17. **crux** (kruks) n.	crucial part of a problem	The **crook** caused a **crucial problem**.
18. **fulsome** (fuul-som) adj.	excessive, disgusting	
19. **benign** (be-nin) adj.	kindly	**Be nice** to **kindly** old ladies.
20. **encumber** (en-kum-ber) v.	to be a burden	Peeling a cucumber is a real burden

polit, polis—city

The **pole** is **lit** above the **city**.

WORD ROOT	MEANING	ASSOCIATION *Where examples are not given, create and write your associations in the spaces provided!*
POLIT, POLIS	**city**	The **pole** is **lit** above the **city**.
politics (pol-i-tiks) n.	science and art of governing, whether a city or country.	
politician (pol-i-tish-an) n.	a person engaged to govern.	
cosmopolitan (koz-mo-pol-i-tan) adj.	of many parts of the world, containing people from many countries.	
metropolitan (met-ro-pol-i-tan) adj.	of a metropolis.	
metropolis (me-trop-o-lis) n.	chief city of country or region.	
police (po-lees) n.	civil force responsible for keeping order in public.	
DEM, DEMO	**people**	______________________
democracy (de-mok-ra-see) n.	governed by the people, especially through representatives they elect.	
demography (di-mog-ra-fee) n.	scientific study of population statistics.	
antidemocratic (an-ty-dim-a-kra-tik) n.	opposed to rule by the people.	
demagogue (dem-a-gawg) n.	leader who wins support with emotional appeal rather than reasoning.	
demotic (di-mot-ik) adj.	of ordinary people.	
demotist (di-moh-tist) n.	one who reduces another to a lower rank or category.	
CIV	**citizen**	All the **citizens** met at the **civic** center.
civic (siv-ik) adj.	proper to citizens, or to a city or town.	
civilian (si-vil-yan) n.	private citizen not in military.	
civil (siv-il) adj.	belonging to citizens.	
civilization (siv-i-li-zay-shon) n.	making or becoming civilized.	
uncivilized (un-siv-i-lizd) adj.	not enlightened in civilized behavior.	
decivilize (de-siv-i-lyz) adj.	act of reverting to savage behavior, not socially acceptable.	

REVIEW

Mark the letter of the correct word for each definition in the space provided.

1. **to improve**
   a. personify b. superimpose c. ameliorate ___C___
2. **flattering speech**
   a. ephemeral b. blandishment c. proboscis ___B___
3. **agent of revenge**
   a. nemesis b. philanthropist c. surrogate ___A___
4. **daily**
   a. antebellum b. diurnal c. incipient ___B___
5. **kindly**
   a. blatant b. benign c. sedentary ___B___
6. **conversation**
   a. colloquy b. conjecture c. circumvent ___A___
7. **of ordinary people**
   a. acrimony b. demotic c. facetious ___B___
8. **crucial part of a problem**
   a. crux b. atoll c. node ___A___
9. **dilemma**
   a. quandary b. pedagogue c. wraith ___A___
10. **non-military citizen**
    a. misanthrope b. civilian c. piquant ___B___

Mark the letter or write the word that best completes each sentence.

1. Just before final exams, most students study at a ___frentic___ pace.
   a. limpid b. frenetic c. affable
2. Wars are won by the actions of ___intrepid___ soldiers.
   a. intrepid b. corpulent c. impotent
3. Segregated communities contain people with ___homogeneous___ viewpoints.
   a. intravenous b. synthetic c. homogeneous
4. Many writers who strive for greatness achieve ___banal___ results instead.
   a. banal b. irascible c. vehement
5. The widow preferred not to ___encumber___ her relatives with requests.
   a. explicate b. encumber c. transcend
6. People who are obese have a ___fulsome___ diet.
   a. incestuous b. skeptical c. fulsome
7. Most systems of philosophy are based on ___dialectic___ thought.
   a. dialectic b. ventricle c. inertia
8. People who travel a lot have a ___cosmopolitan___ air about them.
   a. sordid b. dynastic c. cosmopolitan
9. A withered old woman is often called a ___crone___.
   a. scrivener b. crone c. maelstrom
10. There is nothing like a ___poignant___ love story to make people cry.
    a. poignant b. facile c. prevalent
11. Students with higher degrees often use ___erudite___ language.
    a. palpable b. erudite c. commensurate
12. A literary ___motif___ is a recurring theme.
    a. tapir b. compendium c. motif
13. An audience watching a farce leaves the theater with the sound of a ___guffaw___.
    a. guffaw b. lament c. parry

10

menagerie (me-naj-e-ree)—collection of wild animals in captivity
See the **manager** of the **wild animals**.

EXAMPLE OF USE

1. A zoo is a **menagerie.**
2. After the argument, he **proffered** his hand in friendship.
3. The ballerina executed a perfect **arabesque.**
4. In these inflationary times, it makes good sense to be **frugal.**
5. Out of defiance she abandoned the sidesaddle to **bestride** the horse instead.
6. The only **remuneration** he received for his volunteer work was the satisfaction of helping others.
7. I find the task of punishing you most **odious**, but necessary.
8. For such a young, inexperienced person, he possesses remarkable **aplomb.**
9. Most gambling casinos use some form of **scrip** instead of cash.
10. In many primitive tribes, the sole leader and lawmaker is the **patriarch.**
11. Extra care should be taken in the **nurturing** of young seedlings.
12. I must **remonstrate** about the lack of police protection in this area.
13. The staff of the hospital is grateful for the **beneficence** of the volunteer workers.
14. Since they couldn't settle the dispute between themselves, they decided on **adjudication.**
15. The desert has a **salutary** climate for those with respiratory problems.
16. This was a very **palatable** meal, or else I was just very hungry.
17. There is a **disparity** between what the records show and what's actually in our petty cash box.
18. Our library **archives** contain some very rare letters.
19. Please do not **sully** the air with your swearing.
20. When garbage begins to **putrefy**, you can usually tell right away.

A man doesn't know what he knows until he knows what he doesn't know.
—Thomas Carlyle

WORD	DEFINITION	ASSOCIATION *Where examples are not given, create and write your associations in the spaces provided!*
1. **menagerie** (me-naj-e-ree) n.	collection of wild animals in captivity	See the **manager** in charge of the **wild animals**.
2. **proffer** (prof-er) v.	to offer	The proffersor offered.
3. **arabesque** (ar-a-besk) n.	architectural design, ballet position	See the **Arab mosque** is of a beautiful **architectural design**.
4. **frugal** (froo-gal) adj.	careful & economical; costing little	__________
5. **bestride** (bi-stride) v.	to mount with legs astride	I **mounted** the horse for the **best ride** of my life.
6. **remuneration** (ri-myoo-ne-ray-shun) n.	compensation	__________
7. **odious** (oh-di-us) adj.	hateful; disgusting	Oh!, **de odor is** so **disgusting**.
8. **aplomb** (a-plom) n.	self-confidence; dignity	With dignity he told us he had planted a blomb.
9. **scrip** (skrip) n.	paper, with promise to pay	With this **scrap** of paper I **promise to pay** you.
10. **patriarch** (pay-tri-ahrk) n.	male head of family or tribe	__________
11. **nurture** (nur-chur) v.	to feed; bring up	We will **bring up** our children to be **mature**.
12. **remonstrate** (ri-mon-strayt) v.	to protest	__________
13. **beneficence** (be-nef-i-sens) n.	an act of kindness	See, it **benefits** all to **be kind**!
14. **adjudicate** (a-joo-di-kayt) v.	to decide; act as judge	__________
15. **salutary** (sal-yu-ter-ee) adj.	healthful; producing a wholesome effect	**Solitary** meditation can produce a **healthy effect**.
16. **palatable** (pal-a-ta-bel) adj.	pleasant to the taste or mind	__________
17. **disparity** (di-spar-i-tee) n.	difference; inequality	They **despaired** at their **differences**.
18. **archives** (ahr-kivz) n.	place where records are kept	__________
19. **sully** (sul-ee) v.	to soil; tarnish; spoil the purity of	"**Sully** boy, don't **soil** your clothes."
20. **putrefy** (pyoo-tri-fi) v.	to cause to rot or decay	__________

COLOR THE CHROME BUMPER

chrom—color

See the **color** on the **chrome** bumper of the car.

WORD ROOT	MEANING	ASSOCIATION *Where examples are not given, create and write your associations in the spaces provided!*
CHROM	**color**	See the **color** on the **chrome** bumper of the car.
chromatic (kroh-mat-ik) adj.	of colors, in colors.	
chromatography (kroh-ma-tog-ra-fee) n.	separation of mixed substances.	
chromogenesis (kroe-mo-jen-e-sis) n.	color reproduction.	
chromatosis (kroe-ma-toe-sis) n.	unnatural pigmentation, coloring of the skin.	
achromatic (a-kroh-mat-ik) adj.	having no color.	
orthochromatic (or-tho-kroh-mat-ik) adj.	correctly blended colors.	
VIS, VID	**see**	____________________
visual (vizh-oo-al) adj.	of or used in seeing.	
vision (vizh-on) n.	faculty of sight.	
visage (viz-ij) n.	a person's face.	
vista (vis-ta) n.	a view, seen and appreciated.	
invisible (in-viz-i-bel) adj.	unable to be seen.	
evident (ev-i-dent) adj.	obvious to the eye or mind.	
AUD, AUS	**hear, listen**	**Hear** how quiet my new **Audi** drives.
audio (aw-di-oh) n.	sound that is heard.	
audience (aw-di-ens) n.	people gathered to hear or watch something.	
audiphone (au-di-fone) n.	a hearing aid.	
auscultation (aw-skul-tay-shun) n.	the act of listening to sounds in chest, abdomen, etc.	
inaudible (in-aw-di-bel) adj.	unable to be heard.	
audition (aw-dish-on) n.	trial to test the ability of a prospective performer.	

REVIEW

Draw a line between the word and its correct definition.

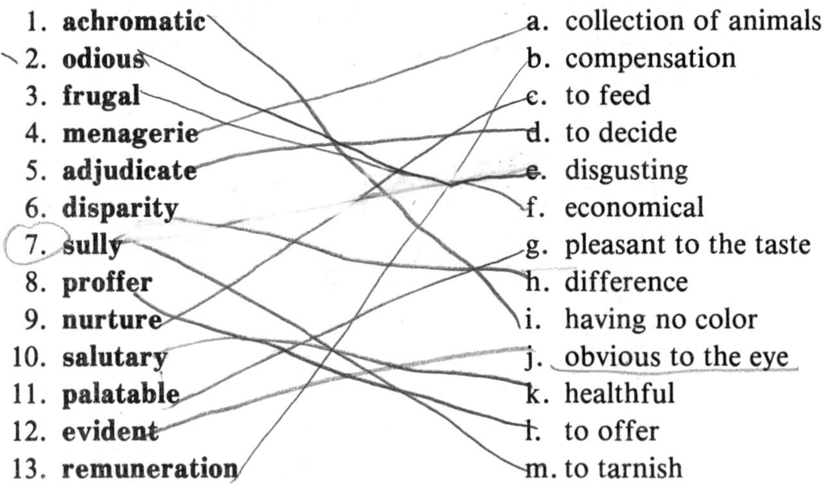

1. **achromatic**	a. collection of animals
2. **odious**	b. compensation
3. **frugal**	c. to feed
4. **menagerie**	d. to decide
5. **adjudicate**	e. disgusting
6. **disparity**	f. economical
7. **sully**	g. pleasant to the taste
8. **proffer**	h. difference
9. **nurture**	i. having no color
10. **salutary**	j. obvious to the eye
11. **palatable**	k. healthful
12. **evident**	l. to offer
13. **remuneration**	m. to tarnish

Circle the correct word below each definition.

1. **to mount with legs astride**
   (prevaricate, dismember, bestride, maladroit)
2. **cause to rot**
   (nihilistic, putrefy, emollient, irradiate)
3. **to protest**
   (remonstrate, circumspect, placate, impinge)
4. **hearing aid**
   (audition, audiphone, autocrat, autonomous)
5. **paper with promise to pay**
   (script, scripture, scrap, scrip)
6. **male head of the family**
   (patrician, paramour, patriarch, protagonist)
7. **self-confidence**
   (osculation, inebriate, aplomb, necromancy)
8. **act of kindness**
   (diatribe, beneficence, transfiguration, expatriate)
9. **ballet position**
   (narcosis, grippe, arabesque, vermilion)
10. **place where records are kept**
    (armory, archives, archetype, arbiter)

11

chagrin (sha-grin)—a feeling of embarrassment
She grinned when **embarrassed**.

EXAMPLE OF USE

1. Much to his **chagrin**, he was overheard making disparaging remarks about his boss.
2. These diet pills will act as a **quietus** on your appetite.
3. The Constitution talks of providing for the "common **weal.**"
4. There are times when I would like to retire to some remote **atoll** in the Pacific.
5. In Biblical times, the Israelites' **exodus** from Egypt represented an early triumph for the cause of freedom.
6. Some archaeologists think civilization began at the **delta** of the Nile River.
7. His doctor pronounced him **hale** and hearty.
8. When a plant **atrophies,** it usually is dying.
9. The lambs were **gamboling** across the meadow.
10. The horse kept going around the track at a steady **canter**.
11. He **curried** the king's favor with compliments and lies.
12. The king was **bewitched** by her beauty and granted her wish.
13. It's not within my **ken** to predict the future.
14. I can **attest** to the fact that you were with me that day.
15. He could not **educe** a hypothesis from the data given.
16. The **august** presence of the aging monarch forced the young servant to his knees.
17. Some critics suspect that evil **machinations** behind the scenes are shaping our international policy.
18. When his debt was finally paid off, he received his **quittance**.
19. Although the committee members came from **diverse** walks of life, they were united in a common purpose.
20. Our land **abuts** a municipal dump.

The thoughtless are rarely wordless.
—Howard W. Newton

WORD	DEFINITION	ASSOCIATION *Where examples are not given, create and write your associations in the spaces provided!*
1. **chagrin** (sha-grin) n.	a feeling of embarrassment	**She grinned** when embarrassed.
2. **quietus** (kwi-ee-tus) n.	death	
3. **weal** (weel) n.	well-being	
4. **atoll** (at-awl) n.	ring-shaped coral reef that encloses lagoon	See paying **a toll** to cross the **coral reef enclosing the lagoon.**
5. **exodus** (ek-so-dus) n.	departure, usually of many people	
6. **delta** (del-ta) n.	mouth of river	
7. **hale** (hayl) adj.	healthy & strong	To **hail** a taxi in New York takes a **strong** and **healthy** voice!
8. **atrophy** (at-ro-fee) v.	to waste away from lack of use	
9. **gambol** (gam-bol) v.	jump or skip about in play	
10. **canter** (kan-ter) n.	a gentle gallop	That horse **can turn** even while **gently galloping**.
11. **curry** (kur-ee) v.	seek favor by flattery; groom a horse; seasoning	
12. **bewitch** (bi-wich) v.	to charm	
13. **ken** (ken) n.	range of vision or knowledge	**Ken** has amazing **knowledge** on the subject of **vision**.
14. **attest** (a-test) v.	confirm; declare to be true	
15. **educe** (i-doos) v.	draw or bring out	
16. **august** (aw-gust) adj.	majestic, imposing	During **August** the heat is **imposing** and the sunset's **majestic**.
17. **machination** (mach-i-nay-shon) n.	clever scheming	
18. **quittance** (kwit-ans) n.	discharge from debt	
19. **diverse** (di-verz) adj.	several; various	See **several divers** looking for **various** treasures.
20. **abut** (a-but) v.	to touch; have a common boundary	

cyclo—wheel, circle

The **motorcycle** goes in **circles**.

WORD ROOT	MEANING	ASSOCIATION *Where examples are not given, create and write your associations in the spaces provided!*
CYCLO	**wheel, circle**	The **motorcycle** goes in **circles**.
bicycle (bi-si-kel) n.	two-wheeled vehicle driven by pedals.	
cyclical (sik-lik-ul) adj.	recurring in cycles or series.	
encyclopedia (en-si-klo-pee-dee-a) n.	a book or set of books giving information about all branches of knowledge.	
cyclone (si-klohn) n.	around a calm central area.	
cyclitis (si-kli-tis) n.	of the eyelashes.	
cyclops (si-klops) n.	mythical giant with one circular eye in the middle of the forehead.	
CIRCUM, CIRC	**around**	________________
circumstance (sur-kum-stans) n.	one of the conditions or facts connected with an event or person.	
circuit (sur-kit) n.	a line or route or distance around a place.	
circumference (sur-kum-fe-rens) n.	the boundary of a circle, the distance around this.	
circumspect (sur-kum-spekt) adj.	cautious and watchful, wary.	
circumnavigate (sur-kum-nav-i-gayt) v.	to sail completely around.	
circumvent (sur-kum-vent) v.	to evade, to find a way around.	
MEDI	**half, middle, between**	________________
medium (meed-ee-um) n.	a middle stage or degree, mean.	
mediocrity (mee-dee-ok-re-tee) n.	the quality or state of being ordinary.	
mediterranean (med-i-te-ran-e-un) n.	having land on all sides.	
medieval (med-ee-val) adj.	belonging to the Middle Ages.	
mediator (mee-di-ay-tor) n.	acting as negotiator.	
median (mee-di-an) n.	a point or line, etc., situated in the middle.	

REVIEW

Mark true or false in the space provided.

1. ________ A **delta** is the mouth of a river.
2. ________ An **atoll** is a guard gate between national boundaries.
3. ________ To **attest** to a set of facts is to disagree.
4. ________ **Mediocrity** is the achievement of greatness.
5. ________ To **gambol** is to skip about in play.
6. ________ A man with **diverse** talents can do many jobs.
7. ________ The common **weal** refers to complaints from the populace.
8. ________ A feeling of **chagrin** is akin to embarrassment.
9. ________ A **cyclops** is a vehicle that can fly.
10. ________ An **august** occasion is a time for wearing old clothes.

Mark the letter from column 2 that best describes each word in column 1.

1		2
abut	________	a. to charm
atrophy	________	b. death
exodus	________	c. strong
canter	________	d. clever scheming
circumvent	________	e. discharge from debt
quietus	________	f. departure to another land
hale	________	g. a gentle gallop
ken	________	h. to have a common boundary
quittance	________	i. to seek favor
machination	________	j. to waste away
bewitch	________	k. to bring out
curry	________	l. range of vision
educe	________	m. to evade a situation

12

forte (fort)—person's strong point

See the **fort** is the **strong point** of the city.

EXAMPLE OF USE

1. French cuisine isn't my **forte**; I'm much better at cooking Italian dishes.

2. The **dichotomy** between the two sides in the conflict may never be reconciled.

3. Your bank statement shows **accrued** interest in the amount of $125.

4. I like city life and can't understand how some people prefer to **rusticate** in the suburbs.

5. The **lachrymal** quality to sad, old ballads may in part account for their enduring popularity.

6. A **tankard** of ale was considered a treat by Robin Hood and his men.

7. Static has caused the broadcast to be **garbled**.

8. The job was **beset** by problems from start to finish.

9. After the hurricane, the city was a **shambles**.

10. Mosquitoes are very common in Louisiana because they breed in the **bayous**.

11. The lawyer said this testimony was not **germane** to the case under consideration.

12. His **mien** was serious, as befitted a clergyman.

13. The book, *Pilgrim's Progress*, is an **allegory** of the temptations and victories of man's soul.

14. The wrong kind of gossip can be **deleterious** to one's reputation.

15. A missing piece of information caused a **hiatus** in our research.

16. He gave the book only a **cursory** glance because he wasn't really interested in it.

17. Fear made her voice **tremulous**.

18. Those who **scoff** at parking tickets may be in big trouble when their sins catch up with them.

19. Now we have to face the **onerous** task of tabulating the census.

20. The incidence of bronchial trouble in London may be related to the **dank** climate.

Words are one of our chief means of adjusting to all the situations of life. The better control we have over words, the more successful our adjustment is likely to be. —Bergen Evans

WORD	DEFINITION	ASSOCIATION *Where examples are not given, create and write your associations in the spaces provided!*
1. **forte** (fort) n.	person's strong point	See the **fort** is the **strong point** of the city.
2. **dichotomy** (di-kot-o-mee) n.	division into two parts	______
3. **accrue** (a-kroo) v.	accumulate	______
4. **rusticate** (rus-ti-kayt) v.	to settle in the country	See **rusty gates settling** all over **the countryside**.
5. **lachrymal** (lak-ri-mal) adj.	of tears	______
6. **tankard** (tang-kard) n.	large drinking cup	______
7. **garble** (gahr-bel) v.	to give a confused account of, distort	He gave a **confused, distorted account** of how **tar** got on the **bell**.
8. **beset** (be-set) v.	to surround	______
9. **shambles** (sham-belz) n.	scene of great bloodshed, disorder	______
10. **bayou** (bi-oo) n.	marshy body of water	Can I **buy you** that **marshy body of water** over there?
11. **germane** (jer-mayn) adj.	relevant	______
12. **mien** (me-en) n.	a person's manner	______
13. **allegory** (al-e-gohr-ee) n.	symbolic story with deeper meaning	**All the gory symbols** give that story **deeper meaning**.
14. **deleterious** (del-e-teer-i-us) adj.	harmful to body or mind	______
15. **hiatus** (hi-ay-tus) n.	a break or gap in a series	______
16. **cursory** (kur-so-ree) adj.	superficial, not thorough	See the boss **curse me** for doing a **superficial** and **unthorough** job.
17. **tremulous** (trem-yu-lus) adj.	trembling, quivering	______
18. **scoff** (skof) v.	ridicule	______
19. **onerous** (on-e-rus) adj.	burdensome	The **owner of us** horses has a **burdensome** responsibility.
20. **dank** (dangk) adj.	unpleasantly damp and cold	______

a, an—not, without

See the teacher say "there is **not** and we are **without** a letter before the letter **'a'** in the alphabet."

WORD ROOT	MEANING	ASSOCIATION *Where examples are not given, create and write your associations in the spaces provided!*
A, AN	**not, without**	See the teacher say "there is **not** and we are **without** a letter before the letter **'a'** in the alphabet."
amorphous (a-mor-fus) adj.	having no definite shape or form.	
apathetic (ap-a-thet-ik) adj.	lack of interest or concern.	
anemia (a-nee-mi-a) n.	lack of red corpuscles in blood.	
anecdote (an-ik-doht) n.	short story about real person or event.	
anonymous (a-non-i-mus) adj.	name not made public.	
anesthesia (an-is-thee-zha) n.	loss of sensation.	
UN	**not**	______________________
unknown (un-nohn) adj.	not known, not identified.	
uneducated (un-ej-u-kay-tid) adj.	not educated, ignorant.	
unwelcome (un-well-kum) adj.	not welcome, not wanted.	
unloved (un-luvd) adj.	not loved or cared for.	
unable (un-ay-bel) adj.	not able.	
unfinished (un-fin-isht) adj.	not finished.	
NON	**not**	______________________
nonsense (non-sens) n.	talk or idea that is absurd, foolish.	
nonstop (non-stop) adj.	without stopping or pausing.	
nonconformist (non-kon-for-mist) n.	person who does not conform to established principles.	
nonprofit (non-prof-it) adj.	not established for making money.	
nontoxic (non-toks-ik) adj.	contains no harmful particles.	
nonsequitur (non-sek-wi-tur) adv.	Latin: it does not follow.	

REVIEW

Mark the letter of the correct word for each definition in the space provided.

1. **harmful to body or mind** ______
   a. permeable b. indomitable c. deleterious
2. **tearful** ______
   a. loquacious b. lachrymal c. lascivious
3. **to settle in the country** ______
   a. residual b. reconnoiter c. rusticate
4. **a person's manner** ______
   a. mien b. moribund c. macrocosm
5. **to accumulate** ______
   a. accost b. acclimate c. accrue
6. **division into two parts** ______
   a. duodenum b. dichotomy c. diminutive
7. **trembling** ______
   a. tremulous b. tertiary c. trenchant
8. **a person's strong point** ______
   a. forte b. prospectus c. strophe
9. **having no definite shape** ______
   a. affable b. amorphous c. anthropomorphic
10. **person who doesn't follow established principles** ______
    a. nomenclature b. nocturn c. nonconformist

Mark the letter or write the word that best completes each sentence.

1. The innkeeper lifted a large ______ of beer to the bar.
   a. poultice b. tankard c. scion
2. The marshlands of Louisiana are known as ______ country.
   a. bagatelle b. fistula c. bayou
3. The dispatcher was known to ______ the message in transmission.
   a. flagellate b. garble c. misanthrope
4. Earning a living is often an ______ task.
   a. onerous b. acephalous c. effluent
5. That information is not ______ to the subject.
   a. impuissant b. germane c. tactual
6. Such hoodlums are ______ in polite society.
   a. underscored b. unctuous c. unwelcome
7. After the robbery the apartment was in a ______.
   a. fanfaronade b. shambles c. niche
8. The new company was ______ by problems with creditors.
   a. benign b. beset c. consummate
9. The stunt man was on ______ between films.
   a. hegemony b. waiver c. hiatus
10. The weathered castle was a ______, dark shelter for the night.
    a. tepid b. fecund c. dank
11. *Moby Dick* is more than a fish story; it is an ______ of human nature.
    a. adversary b. allegation c. allegory
12. The student failed the test after a ______ review of the text.
    a. cadaverous b. cursory c. culpable
13. People with talent tend to ______ at those who don't.
    a. emulate b. genuflect c. scoff

13

eschew (es-shoo)—to avoid

If someone throws **a shoe** at you, duck to **avoid** it!

EXAMPLE OF USE

1. Vegetarians **eschew** meat and meat by-products.
2. With great **agility** he leaped out of the way of the oncoming car.
3. This money has been **allocated** for special educational projects.
4. The king celebrated the birth of his first child by granting **amnesty** to all prisoners.
5. The coming of winter **evokes** memories of sleds, heavy coats, and heating bills.
6. An attempt has been made to **impeach** the senator with charges of accepting bribes.
7. He is a man of great **affluence**; therefore, he does not stop to ask how much anything costs.
8. This vase is **unique**; I'm sure there isn't another one like it anywhere.
9. There's something **sinister** going on in that old boarded-up house.
10. The robber **coerced** the bank teller into opening the vault.
11. The amount of interest has been **computed** by our loan department.
12. Will you please **validate** my parking ticket?
13. The little boy **badgered** his mother into letting him stay up late.
14. I **advocate** equal pay for equal work.
15. It used to be more common for police to **harass** suspects; now their powers have been limited by the Constitution.
16. What began as a minor disagreement led to a permanent **rift** in their relations.
17. The prospect of moving to a new town can cause **regressive** behavior in young children.
18. A famous archaeological **hoax** involved a so-called Candiff Giant.
19. We thought we saw a lake in the distance, but it turned out to be a **mirage**.
20. The police have had the suspect's house under 24-hour **surveillance**.

From a man's mouth you can tell who he is.
—Zohar

WORD	DEFINITION	ASSOCIATION *Where examples are not given, create and write your associations in the spaces provided!*
1. **eschew** (es-shoo) v.	to avoid	If someone throws **a shoe** at you, duck to **avoid** it!
2. **agility** (a-jil-it-ee) n.	quickness, nimbleness	______
3. **allocate** (al-o-kayt) v.	to set aside, to apportion, to allot	______
4. **amnesty** (am-ne-stee) n.	pardon	**I'm nasty** you know, please **pardon** me.
5. **evoke** (i-voek) v.	to call up or produce	______
6. **impeach** (im-peech) v.	to accuse, question	______
7. **affluence** (af-loo-ens) n.	wealth	**Wealthy** people have lots of **influence**.
8. **unique** (yoo-neek) adj.	one of a kind; without an equal	______
9. **sinister** (sin-i-ster) adj.	evil	______
10. **coerce** (koh-urs) v.	to force	See the similar spelling—change **coerce** to **foerce**!
11. **compute** (kom-pyoot) v.	calculate	______
12. **validate** (val-i-dayt) v.	confirm	______
13. **badger** (baj-er) v.	to tease, nag	See the **badger** get angry when you **tease** and **nag** him.
14. **advocate** (ad-vo-kayt) v.	to recommend	______
15. **harass** (ha-ras) v.	annoy by repeated attacks	______
16. **rift** (rift) n.	break in friendly relations	See the **friends drift** apart when **relationships break off**.
17. **regressive** (re-gres-iv) adj.	going back	______
18. **hoax** (hohks) n.	joke, plot to trick or deceive	______
19. **mirage** (mi-rahzh) n.	optical illusion	The **mirror's age** is an **optical illusion**; it looks brand new!
20. **surveillance** (sur-vay-lans) n.	supervision	______

port—carry

Into the **port** they **carry** their boat.

WORD ROOT	MEANING	ASSOCIATION *Where examples are not given, create and write your associations in the spaces provided!*
PORT	**carry**	Into the **port** they **carry** their boat.
portable (pohr-ta-bel) adj.	able to be carried.	
transport (trans-pohrt) v.	to carry from one place to another.	
deport (di-pohrt) v.	to remove an unwanted person from a country.	
reporter (ri-pohr-ter) n.	person employed to gather news.	
support (su-pohrt) v.	to bear the weight of.	
import (im-pohrt) v.	to bring in from an outside source.	
LOC, LOCO	**place**	____________________
locale (loh-kal) n.	place of operations or events.	
locomotion (loh-ko-moh-shon) n.	ability to move from place to place.	
locate (loh-kayt) v.	discover the place where something is.	
dislocate (dis-loh-kayt) v.	to put out of place	
relocate (ree-loh-kayt) v.	to move to a different place.	
allocate (al-o-kayt) v.	to give a share.	
GEO, GE	**earth, soil, ground**	____________________
geography (jee-og-ra-fee) n.	scientific study of Earth's surface.	
geology (jee-ol-o-jee) n.	scientific study of Earth's crust and strata.	
geocentric (jee-oh-sen-trik) adj.	considering Earth as a center.	
geodesic (jee-o-des-ik) n.	shortest line between points on a curved surface.	
geomorphic (jee-oh-mor-fik) adj.	study of physical features of Earth's surface.	
geomagnetic (jee-oh-mag-net-ik) adj.	relating to Earth's magnetic properties.	

REVIEW

Draw a line between the word and its correct definition.

1. **agility**	a. optical illusion
2. **badger**	b. to call forth
3. **rift**	c. quickness
4. **hoax**	d. a break in friendship
5. **surveillance**	e. going backwards
6. **regressive**	f. to tease
7. **sinister**	g. a plot to deceive
8. **unique**	h. evil
9. **mirage**	i. one of a kind
10. **evoke**	j. supervision

Circle the correct word below each definition.

1. **to bring in from outside source**
   (potentate, import, brioche, plaudit)
2. **to avoid**
   (eschew, fluctuate, smite, extenuate)
3. **to force**
   (efface, coerce, entice, strumpet)
4. **to accuse**
   (impale, impeach, imprecate, languish)
5. **ability to move from place to place**
   (static, locomotion, latent, corporeal)
6. **to set aside**
   (altercate, allocate, alliterate, assimilate)
7. **wealth**
   (agnosticism, adversity, affluence, aesthetics)
8. **study of the Earth's crust**
   (geophysics, geology, geothermal, geometry)
9. **annoy repeatedly**
   (harass, mitigate, propagate, relegate)
10. **to confirm**
    (vindicate, vacillate, validate, vociferate)
11. **pardon**
    (plethora, amnesty, ignominy, epigram)
12. **to recommend**
    (implicate, advocate, extricate, annihilate)
13. **determine an amount**
    (euphonize, intersect, compute, gormandize)

14

nugatory (noo-ga-tohr-ee)—worthless
See the darn **nuggets** are **worthless**!

EXAMPLE OF USE

1. This agreement is **nugatory**, since no court will enforce it.
2. I had planned to get a lot of work done, but my plans went **awry**.
3. His speech was **stilted**, more like a preacher than a teacher.
4. Much as I care about spiritual matters, I am also concerned with more **mundane** problems.
5. She rubbed the fragrant **balm** into her skin.
6. The dog was **ecstatic** at seeing its master come home.
7. You may have to slow down a little because of the **gradient** of the road.
8. In **avoirdupois** weight, the killer whale tips the scales at approximately 18,000 pounds.
9. The **tribulations** of the early American Indians are just beginning to be recognized.
10. The **irascible** old man chased the children away from his house.
11. At the joints of a plant, a **node** appears.
12. The judge made a **sapient** decision when he sentenced the youth to make restitution.
13. The reconciliation of mother and daughter was a **poignant** scene in that movie.
14. Sometimes the **vagaries** of fortune can upset the most carefully laid plans.
15. Please speak up; your voice is barely **audible**.
16. It upsets me to see an animal **cower** before a man.
17. It's fashionable nowadays for women to **gird** their waists with chains of gold or silver.
18. School vacation lasts a **fortnight**.
19. The **sensuous** pleasures of eating a pomegranate must be experienced firsthand.
20. The **purloined** letter turned out to be the evidence we needed, so I'm glad we got it back.

Speaking without thinking is shooting without aiming.
—W.G. Benham, *Proverbs*

WORD	DEFINITION	ASSOCIATION *Where examples are not given, create and write your associations in the spaces provided!*
1. **nugatory** (noo-ga-tohr-ee) adj.	worthless	See the darn **nuggets** are **worthless**!
2. **awry** (a-ri) adj.	wrong	______
3. **stilted** (stil-tid) adj.	stiffly, pompous, formal	______
4. **mundane** (mun-dayn) adj.	dull, routine	**Monday** is always a **dull** and **routine** day.
5. **balm** (bahm) n.	ointment or something that soothes	______
6. **ecstatic** (ek-stat-ik) adj.	feeling intense delight	______
7. **gradient** (gray-di-ent) n.	slope	See the **great ants** on the **slope** of the hill.
8. **avoirdupois** (av-or-du-poiz) n.	weight	______
9. **tribulation** (trib-yu-lay-shon) n.	great troubles	______
10. **irascible** (i-ras-i-bel) adj.	easily angered, irritable	**A raspy bell easily irritates** and **angers** people.
11. **node** (nohd) n.	knoblike swelling	______
12. **sapient** (say-pi-ent) adj.	pretending to be wise	______
13. **poignant** (poin-yant) adj.	keenly felt	See the **point** of a needle is **keenly felt** when touched!
14. **vagary** (va-gar-ee) n.	impulsive ideas	______
15. **audible** (aw-di-bel) adj.	loud enough to be heard	______
16. **cower** (kow-er) v.	cringe in fear	The **coward cringed in fear**.
17. **gird** (gurd) v.	encircle	______
18. **fortnight** (fort-nite) n.	two weeks	______
19. **sensuous** (sen-shoo-us) adj.	pertaining to the senses	See the word **senses** in **sensuous**.
20. **purloin** (pur-loin) v.	to steal	______

mob, mot, mov—move

See the officer tell the **motley mob** to **move**.

WORD ROOT	MEANING	ASSOCIATION *Where examples are not given, create and write your associations in the spaces provided!*
MOB, MOT, MOV	**move**	See the officer tell the **motley mob** to **move**.
mobility (moh-bil-i-tee) n.	movable, not fixed.	
automobile (aw-to-mo-beel) n.	self-moving vehicle.	
demote (di-moht) v.	to reduce to lower rank or category.	
motivation (moh-ti-vay-shon) n.	inspiration that stimulates interest.	
emotional (i-moh-sho-nal) adj.	move to excessive show of feelings.	
immobile (i-moh-bil) adj.	not moving, fixed.	
AD	**to, toward**	______________________
advance (ad-vans) v.	to move forward, to make progress.	
advantage (ad-van-tij) n.	a favorable condition or circumstance.	
advocate (ad-vo-kayt) v.	to be in favor of.	
advise (ad-viz) v.	to give advice to, to recommend.	
administer (ad-min-i-ster) v.	to manage the business affairs of.	
adhere (ad-heer) v.	to remain faithful or stick to.	
RETRO	**backward**	______________________
retrospect (ret-ro-spekt) n.	survey of past times or events.	
retroactive (ret-roh-ak-tiv) adj.	effective as from a past date, backdated.	
retrograde (ret-ro-grayd) adj.	going backward.	
retrogress (ret-ro-gres) v.	to move backward, to deteriorate.	
retrorocket (ret-roh-rok-it) n.	used for slowing spacecraft, rocket that discharges exhaust in opposite direction of main rocket.	
retrofire (ret-roh-fire) v.	to ignite (a retrorocket).	

REVIEW

Mark true or false in the space provided.

1. ________ A **fortnight** is an evening spent away from home.
2. ________ **Avoirdupois** is a system of weights.
3. ________ To be **audible,** one should speak loudly.
4. ________ When circumstances go **awry**, everything goes wrong.
5. ________ An **ecstatic** experience brings on depression.
6. ________ To **purloin** involves a complicated stitch in knitting.
7. ________ A **gradient** is someone who flunks out of school.
8. ________ **Poignant** dramas include lots of bloodshed.
9. ________ A **node** is a form of swelling on the skin.
10. ________ **Tribulation** is a time of rejoicing.

Mark the letter from column 2 that best describes each word in column 1.

1		2
stilted	________	a. dull
gird	________	b. soothing ointment
sensuous	________	c. pretending to be wise
balm	________	d. odd or impulsive conduct
retrospect	________	e. to cringe in fear
nugatory	________	f. worthless
mundane	________	g. encircle
irascible	________	h. survey of past events
sapient	________	i. to lower in rank
vagary	________	j. to stick to something
demote	________	k. stiff, pompous
cowere	________	l. irritable
adhere	________	m. pertaining to the senses

15

expunge (ik-spunj)—to erase
See the **'X' sponge erase** the blackboard.

EXAMPLE OF USE

1. When you reach maturity, you can have the record of any traffic accidents you had as a minor **expunged,** for a price.
2. Just hearing about your adventure gives me a **vicarious** thrill.
3. As part of the **investiture** ceremony for his new office, he was given a gold lapel pin.
4. He was amazed at the number of **astral** bodies revealed by the new telescope.
5. Silver is frequently used for jewelry because of its **ductile** property.
6. The temptation to **revile** our enemies is ever present.
7. **Alimentary** trouble is usually at the root of anemia.
8. **Slothful** students are usually the ones with the lowest grades.
9. I'm asking you to leave the class because of your **opprobrious** behavior.
10. It is a great asset for an actress to have a **mellifluous** voice.
11. She'd be much more convincing if she could stop **simpering** and give us a real smile.
12. We had an **animated** discussion about the pros and cons of a state lottery.
13. She **blithely** waltzed into the room, unaware of the disapproving glances that followed her.
14. The American refused to pay **obeisance** to the Queen of England.
15. You need a priest to **exorcise** a demon.
16. The architect was asked to redesign the **pilasters** on the facade of the new museum.
17. A hula dancer **undulates** to the music.
18. An **adjunct** to a legislative bill is called a rider.
19. We'll hold that decision in **abeyance** until we have more information.
20. I would prefer not to become **embroiled** in legal technicalities.

He rose without a friend, sat down without an enemy.
—Henry Grattan, of Dr. Lucas after a speech in the Irish Parliament

WORD	DEFINITION	ASSOCIATION *Where examples are not given, create and write your associations in the spaces provided!*
1. **expunge** (ik-spunj) v.	to erase	See the **'X' sponge erase** the blackboard.
2. **vicarious** (vo-kair-i-us) adj.	done or experienced by one person through another	______
3. **investiture** (in-ves-ti-char) n.	act of bestowing office or rank	______
4. **astral** (as-tral) adj.	of or from the stars	**Astrology** is studied **from** movement of **the stars.**
5. **ductile** (duk-til) adj.	metal easily molded	______
6. **revile** (ri-vil) v.	to criticize angrily, slander	______
7. **alimentary** (al-i-man-ta-ree) adj.	nourishing	It's **elementary** that good food is **nourishing**.
8. **slothful** (slawth-ful) adj.	lazy	______
9. **opprobrious** (o-proh-bri-us) adj.	showing scorn, abusive	______
10. **mellifluous** (me-lif-loo-us) adj.	sweet sounding	The **melody flew us** into ecstasy with its **sweet sound**!
11. **simper** (sim-per) v.	smile in a silly way	______
12. **animate** (an-i-mayt) v.	to make lively, give life to	______
13. **blithe** (blith) adj.	casual and carefree	Captain **Blye, the casual** guy!
14. **obeisance** (oh-bay-sens) n.	a deep bow or curtsy, show of respect	______
15. **exorcise** (ek-sor-siz) v.	to drive out (an evil spirit) by prayer	______
16. **pilaster** (pi-las-ter) n.	rectangular column projecting from wall	See them **plaster** the **rectangular column** so it **projects from the wall.**
17. **undulate** (un-ju-layt) n.	to move in waves	______
18. **adjunct** (aj-ungkt) n.	assistant	______
19. **abeyance** (a-bay-ans) n.	suspended for a time	See a **bay of ants suspended in time** and don't move.
20. **embroil** (em-broil) v.	involve in argument	______

spec, spect—look at, examine

He needed his **specs** to **look at** and **examine** the **specs** of dust.

WORD ROOT	MEANING	ASSOCIATION *Where examples are not given, create and write your associations in the spaces provided!*
SPEC, SPECT	**look at, examine**	He needed his **specs** to **look at** and **examine** the **specs** of dust.
spectator (spek-tay-tor) n.	person who watches something.	
spectacle (spek-ta-kel) n.	a striking or impressive sight.	
spectacular (spek-tak-yu-lar) adj.	striking, amazing.	
specter (spek-ter) n.	a ghost.	
spectrum (spek-trum) n.	bands of color as seen in a rainbow.	
inspect (in-spekt) v.	to examine a thing closely and carefully.	
METER	**measure**	______________________
speedometer (spi-dom-e-ter) n.	device in vehicle showing speed.	
thermometer (ther-mom-e-ter) n.	instrument that measures temperature.	
seismometer (syz-mom-e-ter) n.	device that shows force and direction of an earthquake.	
barometer (ba-rom-i-ter) n.	instrument that measures atmospheric pressure.	
pedometer (pe-dom-e-ter) n.	device that measures steps walked.	
symmetrical (si-met-ri-kal) adj.	able to be divided into parts of same size and shape, and similar in position.	
OLOGY	**study, word, idea, science, speech doctrine, reason**	______________________
psychology (sy-kol-o-jee) n.	study of the mind and how it works.	
theology (thee-ol-o-jee) n.	study of religion.	
neurology (nuu-rol-o-jee) n.	scientific study of nerve systems.	
ethnology (eth-nol-o-jee) n.	scientific study of human races.	
anthropology (an-thro-pol-o-jee) n.	scientific study of mankind.	
gynecology (gy-ne-kol-o-jee) n.	scientific study of the female reproductive system.	

REVIEW

Mark the letter of the correct word for each definition in the space provided.

1. **to smile in a silly manner**
   a. snigger b. simper c. admonish ______
2. **carefree**
   a. blithe b. adroit c. lithe ______
3. **assistant**
   a. bailiff b. adjunct c. provost ______
4. **to erase**
   a. lapidify b. expunge c. placate ______
5. **easily molded**
   a. ductile b. prehensile c. lugubrious ______
6. **bands of color**
   a. spectacle b. spectrum c. specter ______
7. **nourishing**
   a. alimentary b. integumentary c. narcoleptic ______
8. **study of nerve systems**
   a. necrophilia b. neurology c. numismatics ______
9. **balanced positioning**
   a. symmetrical b. procephalic c. balustrade ______
10. **showing scorn**
    a. mellifluous b. ribaldry c. opprobrious ______

Mark the letter or write the word that best completes each sentence.

1. People without ambition are said to be __________.
   a. gallant b. slothful c. garrulous
2. His vacation plans were held in __________ due to bad weather.
   a. cahoots b. abeyance c. filature
3. The man led an honorable life out of __________ to his family.
   a. obscurantism b. obtrusion c. obeisance
4. The __________ sounds of the orchestra wafted into the night air.
   a. ecclesiastical b. egregious c. mellifluous
5. The __________ of a king is always a ceremonious event.
   a. inductance b. investiture c. intermezzo
6. While surveying the earthquake damage, he noticed a cracked __________ on the exterior wall.
   a. piliform b. pillory c. pilaster
7. The new managers __________ their predecessors as company scapegoats.
   a. reverberate b. revile c. replicate
8. There are specific rites designated to __________ the devil in one possessed.
   a. geniculate b. exhume c. exorcise
9. Music from the cafe would __________ through the streets every night.
   a. eradicate b. undulate c. expiate
10. A __________ thrill cannot be experienced first-hand.
    a. vicarious b. vivacious c. vitriolic
11. The scandal sheets __________ controversy among readers.
    a. emboss b. embroil c. embalm
12. An __________ voyage is out of this world.
    a. astral b. occidental c. aeruginous
13. A great author must know how to __________ his characters.
    a. ambulate b. animate c. amputate

feign (fayn)—to pretend, make false appearance of
See the girl **pretend** to **faint** in the lifeguard's arms!

EXAMPLE OF USE

1. The young lady **feigned** interest in every word her suitor had to say, but her mind was wandering.
2. Unless that noise **abates**, I'm going to call the police.
3. A good actor can display the **gamut** of emotions, from profound happiness to severe depression.
4. He's so **loquacious** that it's hard to get a word in edgewise.
5. I don't do windows; that's **menial** work.
6. While she was waiting she grew **restive**, so she got up and stretched.
7. I **abhor** violence and wish there was less of it on TV.
8. Aspirin is taken to **alleviate** pain.
9. He **amassed** a fortune by swindling innocent tourists.
10. I can **attest** to the fact that he was here when I arrived.
11. He called **blatant** attention to himself by shouting at the top of his voice.
12. Many automatic drying machines remove excess water by means of **centrifugal** force.
13. Tremendous pressure must have formed the **cleft** in that boulder.
14. Congress was **convoked** at the outbreak of the emergency.
15. When anyone tries to compliment her, she tries to **demean** herself.
16. When the soil **erodes**, the land is no longer good for growing food.
17. Our company is adding new dies to shape the **extruded** plastics it manufactures.
18. He was a **fledgling** salesman, so he made a few mistakes.
19. In his grief, he tried to **rend** his clothing.
20. Wouldn't you rather learn by association than by **rote**?

Words should be weighed, not counted.
—Yiddish proverb

WORD	DEFINITION	ASSOCIATION *Now you're on your own! Create and write your associations in the spaces provided!*
1. **feign** (fayn) v.	to pretend, make false appearance of	See the girl **pretend** to **faint** in the lifeguard's arms!
2. **abate** (a-bayt) v.	to lessen; reduce	____________
3. **gamut** (gam-ut) n.	entire range	____________
4. **loquacious** (loh-kway-shus) adj.	talkative	____________
5. **menial** (mee-ni-al) adj.	lowly; degrading	____________
6. **restive** (res-tiv) adj.	impatient; restless	____________
7. **abhor** (ab-hohr) v.	hate, detest	____________
8. **alleviate** (a-lee-vi-ayt) v.	relieve, make less severe	____________
9. **amass** (a-mass) v.	collect; heap up	____________
10. **attest** (a-test) v.	provide clear proof; declare to be genuine	____________
11. **blatant** (blay-tant) adj.	very obvious and unashamed	____________
12. **centrifugal** (sen-trif-yu-gal) adj.	departing from the center	____________
13. **cleft** (kleft) adj.	split; partly divided	____________
14. **convoke** (kon-vohk) v.	call together; assemble	____________
15. **demean** (di-meen) v.	degrade; lower the dignity	____________
16. **erode** (i-rohd) v.	wear away gradually	____________
17. **extrude** (ik-strood) v.	force out	____________
18. **fledgling** (flej-ling) n.	unexperienced	____________
19. **rend** (rend) v.	split, tear apart	____________
20. **rote** (roht) n.	repetition by a fixed procedure	____________

cap, capit—head, chief, leader

See the **cap** on the **chief's head** over on the **ladder**.

WORD ROOT	MEANING	ASSOCIATION *Now you're on your own! Create and write your associations in the spaces provided!*
CAP, CAPIT	**head, chief, leader**	See the **cap** on the **chief's head** over on the **ladder**.
capitol (kap-i-tol) n.	building in which a state or national legislature meets.	
decapitate (di-kap-i-tayt) v.	to remove the head.	
capitulate (ka-pich-u-layt) v.	to surrender.	
captain (kap-tin) n.	person given authority over a group.	
per capita (pur-kap-i-ta)	"for each person."	
caption (kap-shon) n.	heading, or short title.	
CORP, CORPOR	**body**	______________________
corporation (kor-po-ray-shon) n.	a group of people authorized to act as an individual.	
incorporate (in-kor-po-rayt) v.	to form a legal corporation.	
corpulent (kor-pyu-lent) adj.	fat, bulky body.	
corporeal (kor-pohr-i-al) adj.	bodily.	
corpuscle (kor-pu-sel) n.	a red or white cell in the blood.	
corpse (korps) n.	a dead body.	
POP	**people**	______________________
population (pop-yu-lay-shon) n.	total number of people in a city or country.	
popular (pop-yu-lar) adj.	liked by many people.	
depopulate (dee-pop-yu-layt) v.	reduce population of.	
populous (pop-yu-lus) adj.	thickly populated.	
unpopular (un-pop-yu-lar) adj.	not liked by many people.	
populace (pop-yu-las) n.	the people.	

REVIEW

Draw a line between the word and its correct definition.

1. **gamut**	a. tear apart
2. **centrifugal**	b. very obvious
3. **fledgling**	c. degrade
4. **rend**	d. inexperienced
5. **capitulate**	e. impatient
6. **blatant**	f. reduce the number of people
7. **depopulate**	g. surrender
8. **restive**	h. entire range
9. **demean**	i. call together
10. **convoke**	j. departing from the center

Circle the correct word below each definition.

1. **pretend**
   (sepulcher, feign, maudlin, haggle)
2. **declare to be genuine**
   (attest, reciprocate, testudinate, embezzle)
3. **reduce**
   (pejorate, behoove, abate, detonate)
4. **degrading**
   (cucurbitaceous, menial, mutant, mugwump)
5. **talkative**
   (loquacious, puerile, gallinaceous, figurative)
6. **hate**
   (harangue, abhor, expurgate, meander)
7. **repetition of a lesson**
   (mimesis, pallium, rote, profundity)
8. **partly divided**
   (cleft, demiquaver, syllabic, quadrille)
9. **wear away gradually**
   (engender, erode, drivel, penchant)
10. **head up**
    (amass, abrogate, subjugate, permute)
11. **make less severe**
    (opsonize, alleviate, elucidate, effervesce)
12. **force out**
    (extrude, hegira, osculate, gourde)
13. **fat**
    (grippe, corpulent, stoic, jonquil)

17

flag (flag)—to droop, become weak
Picture a **drooping flag**.

EXAMPLE OF USE

1. He had a beer to revive his **flagging** spirits.
2. That was not only a cruel remark, it was **asinine**.
3. It's very **hypocritical** of him to talk about conserving energy while he's using his air conditioner and it's not even that hot outside.
4. The youngster ate the ice cream and cake with **zeal**.
5. We're going to **raze** that building to make way for the new shopping center.
6. In literature, the most famous **proboscis** was that of Cyrano de Bergerac.
7. I thought I smelled fire, but it was just an **olfactory** hallucination.
8. The headlines were **blazoned** across the front page.
9. You can have that book **gratis** if you promise to give it to someone else when you're done.
10. The **unruly** mob had to be dispersed with tear gas.
11. You expect to find **wraiths** in a haunted house.
12. A pure, **limpid** brook ran through his property.
13. Physicians **purged** the poison from his system and saved his life.
14. We had to **jettison** our cargo to keep the ship afloat.
15. She was trying to appear **incognito**, so she wore big sunglasses.
16. Their relationship promised to be as **ephemeral** as a plucked wildflower.
17. Martin Luther wrote a **tract** criticizing the existing church doctrine.
18. I really appreciate the **pithiness** of this writing; I get so tired of rambling articles that don't say anything.
19. Police were called in to **quell** the riot.
20. He likes to listen to music because it gives him a few moments' **respite** from his action-filled schedule.

Speech is power: speech is to persuade, to convert, to compel.
—Emerson

WORD	DEFINITION	ASSOCIATION *Create and write your associations in the spaces provided!*
1. **flag** (flag) v.	to droop, become weak	Picture a **drooping flag**.
2. **asinine** (as-i-nin) adj.	stupid, silly	___
3. **hypocritical** (hip-o-krit-i-kol) adj.	deceiving	___
4. **zeal** (zeel) n.	fervor, enthusiasm	___
5. **raze** (rayz) v.	destroy completely	___
6. **proboscis** (proh-bos-kis) n.	long snout, elephant's trunk	___
7. **olfactory** (ol-fak-to-ree) adj.	concerning the sense of smell	___
8. **blazon** (blay-zon) v.	decorate with heraldic coat of arms, to proclaim	___
9. **gratis** (grat-is) adj & adv.	free of charge	___
10. **unruly** (un-roo-lee) adj.	lawless, disorderly	___
11. **wraith** (rayth) n.	ghost	___
12. **limpid** (lim-pid) adj.	clear	___
13. **purge** (purj) v.	clear of charges	___
14. **jettison** (jet-i-son) v.	throw overboard	___
15. **incognito** (in-kog-ni-toh) adj. & adv.	identity kept secret	___
16. **ephemeral** (i-fem-e-ral) adj.	short-lived	___
17. **tract** (trakt) n.	pamphlet	___
18. **pithy** (pith-ee) adj.	meaty, concise meaning	___
19. **quell** (qwell) v.	put down, quiet	___
20. **respite** (res-pit) n.	rest	___

leg—law
See the long **leg** of the **law**.

WORD ROOT	MEANING	ASSOCIATION *Create and write your associations in the spaces provided!*
LEG	**law**	See the long **leg** of the **law** .
legal (lee-gal) adj.	based on law.	
legitimate (le-jit-i-mit) adj.	in accordance with laws or rules.	
legislation (lej-is-lay-shon) n.	act of passing a law; the laws enacted.	
legacy (leg-a-see) n.	money or article left to someone in a will.	
delegate (del-e-git) n.	person who represents others and acts according to their instruction.	
legislature (lej-is-lay-chur) n.	a country's or state's legislative assembly.	
JUS, JUR	**law**	
justice (jus-tis) n.	just treatment; fairness; legal proceedings.	
juror (joor-or) n.	member of a body of people sworn to give verdict on case in court of law.	
jurisprudence (joor-is-proo-dens) n.	the study of law or part thereof.	
adjustment (ad-just-ment) n.	a settlement that is fair and proper to all parties.	
conjure (kon-jur) v.	to summon to appear; produce in the mind.	
abjure (aj-joor) v.	to renounce under oath.	
JUD, JUDIC	**judge, lawyer**	
judgment (juj-ment) n.	decision of a judge in a court of law.	
judge (juj) n.	public officer who hears and tries cases in a court of law.	
judiciously (joo-dish-us-lee) adv.	to judge wisely.	
prejudice (prej-u-dis) n.	cause harm to someone's rights or claims.	
judicial (doo-dish-al) adj.	of law courts or administration of justice.	
injudicious (in-joo-dish-us) adj.	unwise; lacking discretion.	

REVIEW

Mark true or false in the space provided.

1. ________ A **pithy** remark is something said in poor taste.
2. ________ To be **hypocritical** is to say one thing and mean another.
3. ________ A **wraith** is a floral arrangement for funerals.
4. ________ An **olfactory** experience excites one's sense of smell.
5. ________ An **unruly** crowd often takes the law into its own hands.
6. ________ An **injudicious** decision is a verdict presented in court.
7. ________ To **abjure** is to renounce under oath.
8. ________ To demonstrate **zeal,** one must be excited about something.
9. ________ A **delegate** represents others at a convention.
10. ________ A **proboscis** is a large signpost with current information on it.

Mark the letter from column 2 that best describes each word in column 1.

1		2
tract	________	a. stupid
raze	________	b. to droop
flag	________	c. destroy completely
asinine	________	d. to proclaim
quell	________	e. clear of charges
respite	________	f. rest
limpid	________	g. to quiet down
blazon	________	h. transparent
gratis	________	i. free of charge
purge	________	j. pamphlet
jettison	________	k. throw overboard
incognito	________	l. something that doesn't last
ephemeral	________	m. identity kept secret

18

strident (stri-dent)—loud harsh sounds or noise
See the boy popping his **sTrident** gum very **noisily**.

EXAMPLE OF USE

1. When he's nervous, his voice becomes very **strident**.

2. **Replete** with fresh fruits and vegetables, the dinner would have satisfied a health food fanatic.

3. He has such an **authoritative** manner, it's difficult to have a friendly difference of opinion with him.

4. Most successful **parody** involves comic exaggeration.

5. He's **malingering** so he can miss final exams.

6. Astrologers try to tell the future by studying the **configuration** of the stars.

7. He's so **dogmatic**, he'll never even admit there are two sides to a question.

8. The policeman used his **truncheon** to repel his attacker.

9. The **soliloquy** must be popular with actors who love the sound of their own voices.

10. Some people think a black cat **portends** bad luck.

11. There is only one **tangible** piece of evidence among all the clues we have here.

12. After a day of horseback riding, he felt discomfort in the **breech** portion of his anatomy.

13. The newspaper stories **aggrandized** the event until those who were there didn't recognize it when they read about it.

14. A good storyteller can **regale** an audience for hours.

15. A headache, with its **concomitant** feeling of misery, is usually only temporary.

16. It was an **arduous** task, but worth the trouble.

17. The old nightclub had an air of **decadence**.

18. It's easier to get a favor from somebody when you are **affable**.

19. A good cry can have a **cathartic** effect that is very helpful.

20. You let her buy that expensive dress, so don't **cavil** at the cheap accessories.

The chief virtue that language can have is clearness, and nothing detracts from it so much as the use of unfamiliar words.
—Hippocrates (460?–370? B.C.)

WORD	DEFINITION	ASSOCIATION *Create and write your associations in the spaces provided!*
1. **strident** (stri-dent) adj.	loud harsh sounds or noise	See the boy popping his **sTrident** gum very **noisily**.
2. **replete** (ri-pleet) adj.	well stocked, full	______
3. **authoritative** (a-thor-i-tay-tiv) adj.	commanding	______
4. **parody** (par-o-dee) n.	humorous imitation	______
5. **malinger** (ma-ling-er) v.	pretend sickness	______
6. **configuration** (kon-fig-u-ray-shon) n.	shape, arrangement	______
7. **dogmatic** (dawg-mat-ik) adj.	authoritative	______
8. **truncheon** (trun-chon) n.	policeman's nightstick	______
9. **soliloquy** (so-lil-o-kwee) n.	talking alone	______
10. **portend** (pohr-tend) v.	to warn, foreshadow	______
11. **tangible** (tan-ji-bel) adj.	capable of being touched	______
12. **breech** (breech) n.	back part of body or anything	______
13. **aggrandize** (a-gran-diz) v.	to exaggerate	______
14. **regale** (ri-gayl) v.	to entertain well	______
15. **concomitant** (kon-kom-i-tant) adj.	accompanying	______
16. **arduous** (ahr-joo-us) adj.	difficult, laborious	______
17. **decadence** (dek-a-dens) n.	decay, less worthy	______
18. **affable** (af-a-bel) adj.	friendly, polite	______
19. **cathartic** (ka-thahr-tik) adj.	cleansing	______
20. **cavil** (kav-il) v.	to raise petty objections	______

monstr—show
See the **monster show**.

WORD ROOT	MEANING	ASSOCIATION *Create and write your associations in the spaces provided!*
MONSTR	**show**	See the **monster show**.
demonstrate (dem-on-strayt) v.	to show evidence of.	
remonstrate (ri-mon-strayt) v.	to make a protest.	
undemonstrative (un-de-mon-stra-tiv) adj.	not showing one's emotions.	
monster (mon-ster) n.	large, ugly, imaginary creature.	
monstrous (mon-strus) adj.	like a monster, huge.	
monstrosity (mon-stros-i-tee) n.	a monster-like thing.	
SCOPE	**watch, see**	______________________
telescope (tel-e-skohp) n.	instrument to make distant objects appear larger.	
microscope (mi-kro-skohp) n.	instrument for viewing objects too small for the naked eye.	
periscope (per-i-skohp) n.	instrument for viewing things that are ordinarily out of sight.	
helioscope (hee-lee-o-skohp) n.	instrument to view the sun without eye injury.	
gyroscope (ji-ro-skohp) n.	device which, when spinning fast, keeps direction of axis unchanged.	
stethoscope (steth-o-skohp) n.	instrument for listening to sounds within the body.	
SAT, SATIS	**enough**	______________________
satisfy (sat-is-fy) v.	to give a person enough to make him contented.	
satiate (say-shi-ayt) v.	to satisfy hunger fully.	
sate (sayt) v.	to fill with an excess of something.	
saturate (sach-u-rayt) v.	to cause to accept as much as possible.	
insatiable (in-say-sha-bel) adj.	unable to get enough.	
dissatisfaction (dis-sat-is-fak-shon) n.	lack of contentment.	

REVIEW

Mark the letter of the correct word for each definition in the space provided.

1. **raise petty objections**
   a. cavort b. cavil c. salivate ______
2. **accompanying factor**
   a. concomitant b. contraindication c. compunction ______
3. **pretend sickness**
   a. malign b. malinger c. malevolent ______
4. **to exaggerate**
   a. acquiescent b. aggrandize c. enjoin ______
5. **harsh sounds**
   a. strident b. blasphemous c. calcinatory ______
6. **make a protest**
   a. remonstrate b. pulsate c. supersede ______
7. **instrument to view the sun without eye injury**
   a. gyroscope b. helioscope c. stethoscope ______
8. **policeman's nightstick**
   a. supplicant b. truncheon c. halidom ______
9. **to entertain splendidly**
   a. enervate b. regale c. gibe ______
10. **shape or design of an object**
    a. cadenza b. capillary c. configuration ______

Mark the letter or write the word that best completes each sentence.

1. To unite an entire nation is an ____________ task for any president.
   a. arduous b. impudent c. obsolescent
2. The musical contained a ____________ on the subject of love.
   a. soliloquy b. obliquity c. solipsism
3. People in positions of responsibility tend to be ____________.
   a. docile b. dogmatic c. dissident
4. Bad omens do not ____________ well for the future.
   a. postulate b. palliate c. portend
5. Scholars have an ____________ desire to learn.
   a. insatiable b. impenitent c. indigent
6. Many great civilizations have collapsed into ____________.
   a. macrocosm b. decadence c. proscenium
7. In a court of law one must present ____________ evidence of guilt.
   a. thematic b. tangible c. torrid
8. Celebrities and popular books are always ripe for ____________.
   a. patronage b. parody c. paragon
9. The ____________ of the gun was tucked against the sheriff's shoulder.
   a. breech b. bridle c. brouhaha
10. If people are ____________ on first meeting, one should try to make friends.
    a. arable b. affable c. acrimonious
11. To clear out the closet and toss things away can be a ____________ experience.
    a. carnivorous b. cathartic c. censorial
12. The catered party was ____________ with food and beverages.
    a. detente b. replete c. histrionic
13. The information is reliable because it comes from an ____________ source.
    a. ambient b. aspiring c. authoritative

19

ANOMALY

anomaly (a-nom-a-lee)—something that deviates from the norm
Recognize similar spelling to word **ABNORMAL**, which means **not normal**.

EXAMPLE OF USE

1. Her removal to a smaller office manifested her **abasement.**

2. He was **abashed** by his wife's scandalous behavior at the cocktail party.

3. Some religions require **ablution** before marriage.

4. The child's table manners are **abominable**!

5. The best known **aboriginal** tribe is found in Australia.

6. Constant criticism will **abrade** your self-confidence.

7. Because of his ambivalence about the bill being introduced, the congressman **abstained** from the vote.

8. I don't understand all the excitement about this book; it is **abysmal**!

9. When you move to a higher altitude, it takes time to become **acclimated** to the thinner air.

10. Lemons and limes both have **acidulous** flavor.

11. She has an **affinity** for men with blue eyes.

12. He **affixed** the boat trailer to the rear bumper of his car.

13. The collage is an **agglutination** of thirty different photographs.

14. We **aligned** the chairs in preparation for the wedding ceremony.

15. The Elephant Man was an **anomaly**.

16. The harried mother tried to **appease** her crying child.

17. She **apportioned** the birthday cake to everyone's satisfaction.

18. He asked the jeweler to **appraise** the worth of the diamond ring.

19. Many students **aspire** to a career in law or medicine.

20. Our property tax is high because our home's value was **assessed** at $250,000.

WORD	DEFINITION	ASSOCIATION *Create and write your associations in the spaces provided!*
1. **abasement** (a-bays-ment) n.	lowering of rank or esteem; humiliation	
2. **abash** (a-bash) v.	embarrass or shame	
3. **ablution** (a-bloo-shon) n.	act of washing; ritual of purification	
4. **abominable** (a-bom-i-na-bel) adj.	repugnant; offensive; unpleasant	
5. **aboriginal** (ab-o-rij-i-nal) adj.	earliest; native	
6. **abrade** (a-brayd) v.	wear away; erode	
7. **abstain** (ab-stayn) v.	refrain voluntarily	
8. **abysmal** (a-biz-mal) adj.	without boundary or end; extreme	
9. **acclimate** (ak-li-mayt) v.	adapt; get used to, especially a new climate	
10. **acidulous** (a-sij-u-lis) adj.	acidy; sour; tart; sarcastic	
11. **affinity** (a-fin-i-tee) n.	natural liking for; similarity	
12. **affix** (a-fiks) v.	fasten, attach or join to	
13. **agglutination** (a-gloo-ti-nay-shon) n.	joining together of distant parts	
14. **align** (a-lin) v.	put in a straight line; join as an ally	
15. **anomaly** (a-nom-a-lee) n.	something that deviates from the norm	Recognize similar spelling to word **ABNORMAL,** which means **not normal**.
16. **appease** (a-peez) v.	to pacify; soothe by making concessions	
17. **apportion** (a-pohr-shon) v.	distribute proportionally; divide into shares	
18. **appraise** (a-prayz) v.	estimate the value of	
19. **aspire** (a-spir) v.	have a goal; ambitious	
20. **assess** (a-ses) v.	evaluate; judge; set charge as for tax	

biblio, bibl—book
A **Bible** is a **book**.

WORD ROOT	MEANING	ASSOCIATION *Create and write your associations in the spaces provided!*
BIBLIO, BIBL	**book**	A **Bible** is a **book.**
bibliophile (bib-li-o-file) n.	lover and collector of books.	
bibliography (bib-li-og-ra-fee) n.	list of books or articles.	
bibliomaniac (bib-li-o-may-nee-ak) n.	collector of books to an extreme.	
Bible (by-bel) n.	a book regarded as authoritative.	
biblical (bib-li-kal) adj.	of or in the Bible.	
SOPH	**wisdom**	__________________________________
philosopher (fi-los-o-fer) n.	an expert in philosophy.	
sophisticated (so-fis-ti-kay-tid) adj.	life and ways lacking natural simplicity.	
sophist (sof-ist) n.	a quibbler.	
sophism (sof-iz-em) n.	false argument intended to deceive.	
sophomore (sof-o-mohr) n.	second year student, a little wiser.	
sophiology (sof-i-ol-o-ji) n.	the science of human ideas.	
DIC, DICT	**say, declare**	__________________________________
dictionary (dik-sho-ner-ee) n.	a book listing words of a language.	
dictator (dik-tay-tor) n.	ruler with unrestricted authority.	
diction (dik-shon) n.	person's manner of speaking words.	
indict (in-dyt) v.	to charge with a crime.	
malediction (mal-e-dik-shon) n.	a curse.	
contradict (kon-tra-dikt) v.	to declare that what is said is untrue.	

REVIEW

Draw a line between the word and its correct definition.

1. **abasement**	a. act of washing
2. **abrade**	b. to have a goal
3. **abash**	c. evaluate
4. **ablution**	d. joining distinct parts
5. **acidulous**	e. from the beginning
6. **affix**	f. wear away
7. **agglutination**	g. to embarrass
8. **anomaly**	h. soothe by making concessions
9. **assess**	i. sour or sarcastic
10. **aspire**	j. humiliation
11. **appease**	k. to join as an ally
12. **align**	l. deviating from the norm
13. **aboriginal**	m. to attach

Circle the correct word below each definition.

1. **offensive**
   (nocturnal, sequester, abominable, erudite)
2. **to get used to**
   (acclimate, aspirate, archetype, amalgamate)
3. **one who loves books**
   (bibliographer, bookmobile, bibliophile, bivouac)
4. **a curse**
   (maladroit, malcontent, malediction, malfeasance)
5. **to estimate the value of something**
   (apprise, expostulate, appraise, defoliate)
6. **to divide into shares**
   (germinate, apportion, espouse, felicitate)
7. **a false argument intended to deceive**
   (solipsism, schism, sophism, mandrill)
8. **refrain voluntarily**
   (abscond, absolve, abstain, abridge)
9. **immeasurable**
   (abrasive, abode, acquisitive, abysmal)
10. **a natural appreciation**
    (admonition, affiliation, affinity, aficionado)

20

bedlam (bed-lam)—place of disruption and confusion, scene of uproar
See **lambs** jumping all over the **bed** causing **uproar** and **confusion**.

EXAMPLE OF USE

1. It is risky to **assume** that your instructions will always be carried out correctly.

2. Because of the parasite, the plant's new leaves grew in long and **attenuated**.

3. Government under the Russian czars was an **autocracy**.

4. When he smiled at the shy girl, she **averted** her eyes.

5. What began as an **avocation** slowly turned into a very profitable business.

6. We expected the worst when we saw the doctor's **baleful** face.

7. The child's recital brought a **beatific** look to his mother's face.

8. In no time at all, the boys had turned the quiet, orderly household into **bedlam**.

9. His boss **berated** him in public for forgetting to send the package.

10. He **beseeched** his wife for forgiveness for getting home so late.

11. Many senior citizens have been **bilked** of their life's savings by con men.

12. The sound of gunshots caused her to **blanch** with fear.

13. The shoemaker used his **bodkin** to poke holes in the leather.

14. That was quite a **boisterous** party you gave!

15. The hiker reached the **bourn** that marked the beginning of private property.

16. Grandpa said, "What a **brash** young man you are to insult me like that!"

17. He sued his partner for **breach** of contract.

18. The professor commented on the **brevity** of her essay and suggested that she expand it.

19. Although she attempted to **bridle** her curiosity, she was unsuccessful.

20. Paintings of **bucolic** landscapes, with shepherds and their flocks, used to be very popular.

It is worse to learn nothing than to know nothing.
—Yiddish Proverb

WORD	DEFINITION	ASSOCIATION *Create and write your associations in the spaces provided!*
1. **assume** (a-soom) v.	take for granted; undertake; put on	______
2. **attenuate** (a-ten-yoo-ayt) v.	reduce in thickness; weaken	______
3. **autocracy** (aw-tok-ra-see) n.	government by one person having unlimited authority	______
4. **avert** (a-vurt) v.	to turn away; ward off	______
5. **avocation** (av-o-kay-shon) n.	hobby; occasional occupation	______
6. **baleful** (bayl-ful) adj.	menacing; destructive	______
7. **beatify** (bi-at-i-fi) v.	make very happy; first step toward church canonization	______
8. **bedlam** (bed-lam) n.	place of disruption and confusion; scene of uproar	See the **lambs** jumping all over the **bed** causing **uproar** and **confusion**.
9. **berate** (be-rayt) v.	scold or chide vehemently	______
10. **beseech** (be-seech) v.	beg	______
11. **bilk** (bilk) v.	cheat or defraud	______
12. **blanch** (blanch) v.	bleach; take the color from	______
13. **bodkin** (bod-kin) n.	small dagger or stiletto, usually for piercing cloth	______
14. **boisterous** (boy-ste-rus) adj.	rowdy; exuberant	______
15. **bourn** (bohrn) n.	boundary; limit; goal	______
16. **brash** (brash) adj.	impetuous; unrestrained; reckless	______
17. **breach** (breech) n.	opening; gap; violation, usually legal or social	______
18. **brevity** (brev-i-tee) n.	shortness; conciseness	______
19. **bridle** (bri-del) n.	restraint or control	______
20. **bucolic** (byoo-kol-ik) adj.	rustic; rural; characteristic of country life	______

auto—self
I bought and drive this **auto** my**self**!

WORD ROOT	MEANING	ASSOCIATION *Create and write your associations in the spaces provided!*
AUTO	**self**	I bought and drive this **auto** my**self**!
automobile (aw-to-mo-beel) n.	a car.	
autograph (aw-to-graf) n.	a person's own signature.	
autonomy (aw-ton-o-mee) n.	self-government.	
autocracy (aw-tok-ra-see) n.	government by one person having unlimited authority.	
automation (aw-to-may-shon) n.	use of automatic equipment to save manual labor.	
automatic (aw-to-mat-ik) adj.	working by itself without human control.	
OPER, OPUS	**work**	______________________
operator (op-e-ray-tor) n.	a person who operates a machine.	
operable (op-e-ra-bel) adj.	able to be operated.	
operate (op-e-rayt) v.	to control the function of.	
cooperation (koh-op-e-ray-shon) n.	work with another.	
opus (oh-pus) n.	musical composition, numbered as one of a composer's works.	
opuscle (oh-pus-kel) n.	small or trivial composition.	
MAN, MANU	**by hand**	______________________
manual (man-yoo-al) adj.	done or operated by hand.	
maneuver (ma-noo-ver) v.	to move something's position carefully.	
manipulate (ma-nip-yu-layt) v.	to handle, manage or use skillfully.	
emancipate (i-man-si-payt) v.	to set free from slavery.	
manifest (man-i-fest) adj.	clear and unmistakable.	
legerdemain (lej-er-de-mayn) n.	sleight of hand, magic tricks.	

REVIEW

Mark true or false in the space provided.

1. ________ To **beatify** someone is to do him great harm.
2. ________ To **avert** danger, one should stay indoors after dark.
3. ________ A **bucolic** existence is to live without hope.
4. ________ An **autocracy** is governed by one absolute ruler.
5. ________ A **bodkin** is a person dressed up in a costume.
6. ________ **Bedlam** is a scene of uproar and confusion.
7. ________ To **blanch** white at the scene of an accident is to grow pale.
8. ________ An **opuscle** is a tendon in the forearm.
9. ________ To **maneuver** a change is to position it deliberately.
10. ________ **Autonomy** is the study of automotive repair.

Mark the letter from column 2 that best describes each word in column 1.

1		2
assume	________	a. restraint
bridle	________	b. impetuous
bourn	________	c. to scold
attenuate	________	d. take for granted
baleful	________	e. hobby
boisterous	________	f. to beg
brash	________	g. rowdy
breach	________	h. boundary
brevity	________	i. to cheat
bilk	________	j. to weaken
avocation	________	k. menacing
berate	________	l. violation, gap
beseech	________	m. shortness

21

choleric (kol-e-rik)—easily angered; often angry

You're **easily** and **often angered** when your shirt **collar** is too tight.

EXAMPLE OF USE

1. The author's short story **burgeoned** into a full-length novel.

2. A **buttress** was built against the weakened wall to support it until repairs could be made.

3. Her **candid** remarks occasionally hurt someone's feelings.

4. The **capacious** station wagon holds nine people.

5. Everyone deplores the horrifying **carnage** of war.

6. Lions are **carnivorous** animals.

7. The man was hired to compile an atlas because he was a master at **cartography**.

8. At the first flash of lightning, his **ceraunophobia** overcame him.

9. Most people are **chary** of door-to-door salesmen.

10. His **choleric** tirades caused her to reconsider her decision to marry him.

11. A **churlish** clerk in a department store may drive customers away.

12. The audience **clamored** for another encore.

13. College students have much to **cogitate** when they study philosophy.

14. We **commiserate** with you, but there's nothing we can do to help.

15. She felt a **compulsion** to buy the dress, even though she did not need it.

16. The business partners made one last effort to **conciliate**, but the bad feelings ran too deep.

17. He would not **condescend** to speak with the group.

18. We should not **condone** his arrogance; that will only make it worse.

19. The private club required that everyone fit the **conformity** of their dress code.

20. The law of gravity is a **constant** in physics.

Clearness is the most important factor in the use of words.
—Quintilian

WORD	DEFINITION	ASSOCIATION *Create and write your associations in the spaces provided!*
1. **burgeon** (bur-jon) v.	blossom; begin to grow rapidly	______
2. **buttress** (but-ris) n.	projecting support of a wall; support or fortify	______
3. **candid** (kan-did) adj.	honest and frank; outspoken	______
4. **capacious** (ka-pay-shus) adj.	roomy; able to hold much	______
5. **carnage** (kahr-nij) n.	killing of many people	______
6. **carnivorous** (kahr-niv-o-rus) adj.	flesh-eating	______
7. **cartography** (kahr-tog-ra-fee) n.	science of drawing maps or charts	______
8. **ceraunophobia** (se-raw-no-fo-bia) n.	irrational fear of thunder and lightning	______
9. **chary** (chair-ee) adj.	cautious; wary	______
10. **choleric** (kol-e-rik) adj.	easily angered; often angry	You're **easily** and **often angered** when your shirt **collar** is too tight.
11. **churlish** (chur-lish) adj.	ill-mannered; rude	______
12. **clamor** (klam-or) n..	loud, prolonged outcry or noise	______
13. **cogitate** (koj-i-tayt) v.	think over; reflect on	______
14. **commiserate** (ko-miz-o-rayt) v.	sympathize; express pity for	______
15. **compulsion** (kom-pul-shon) n.	impulse, usually irresistible	______
16. **conciliate** (kon-sil-i-ayt) v.	pacify; placate; win over	______
17. **condescend** (kon-di-send) v.	assume equality with one believed to be an inferior	______
18. **condone** (kon-dohn) v.	overlook an act or fault without punishment	______
19. **conformity** (kon-for-mi-tee) n.	resemblance; likeness; be in accordance with rules	______
20. **constant** (kon-stant) adj.	not subject to change or variation	______

anthrop—man

See an **ant dropping** on a man.

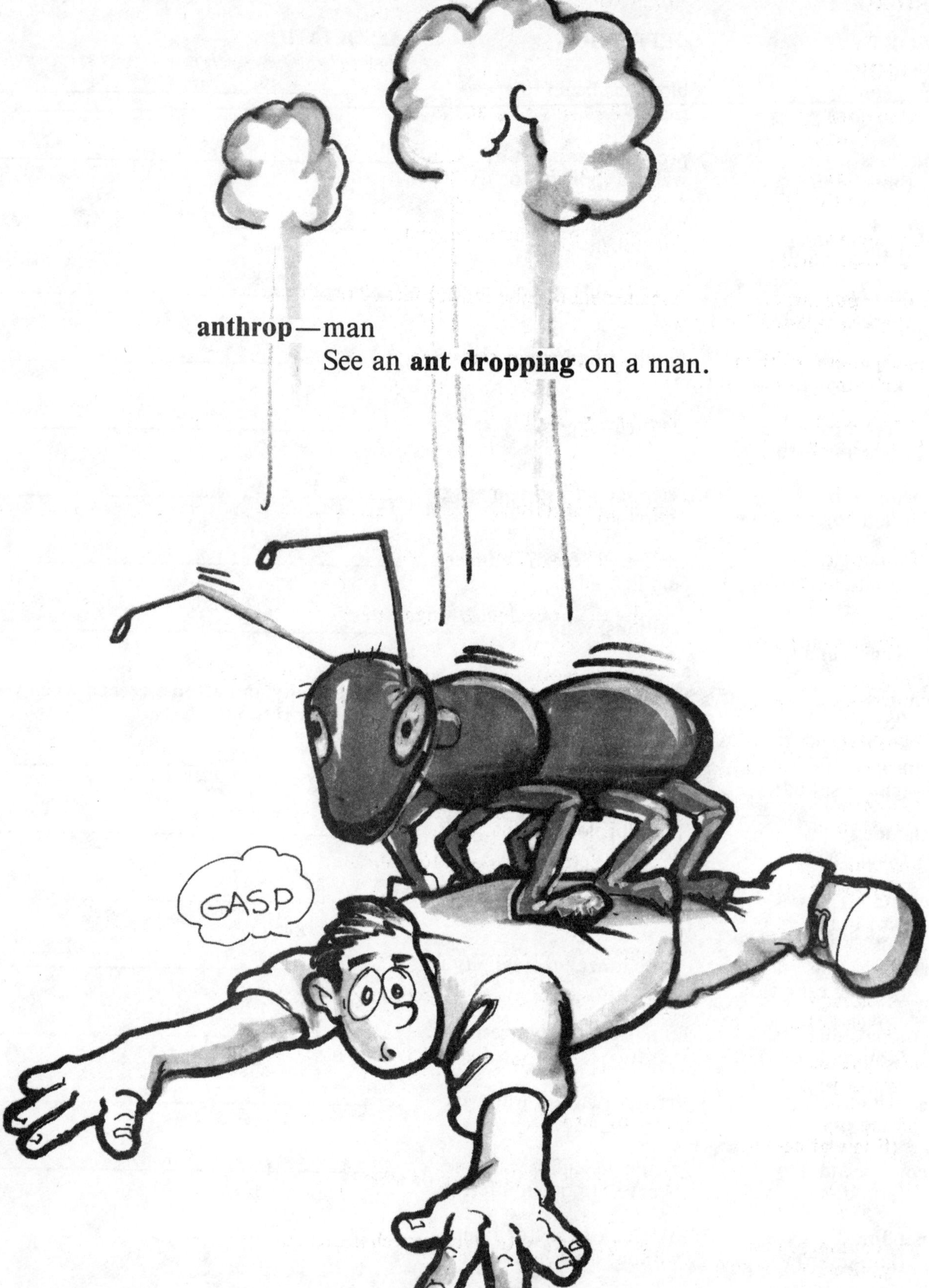

WORD ROOT	MEANING	ASSOCIATION *Create and write your associations in the spaces provided!*
ANTHROP	**man**	See an **ant dropping** on a **man**.
anthropology (an-thro-pol-o-jee) n.	scientific study of mankind.	
philanthropy (fi-lan-thro-pee) n.	love of mankind.	
misanthrope (mis-an-throhp) n.	dislike of mankind in general.	
anthropocentric (an-thro-pe-sen-trik) adj.	assumes man is the central fact of the universe.	
anthropomorphism (an-thro-po-morf-izm) n.	attributing human form to a god, animal or object.	
anthropoid (an-thro-poid) adj.	manlike in form.	
HUM	**earth, ground, man**	____________________
humanities (hyoo-man-i-teez) n.	arts subject as opposed to sciences.	
human (hyoo-man) adj.	having qualities that distinguish mankind from animals.	
inhuman (in-hyoo-man) adj.	brutal, without human qualities of pity and kindness.	
humiliation (hyoo-mil-i-ay-shon) n.	disgrace caused a person.	
exhume (ig-zyoom) v.	to dig up something buried.	
humane (hyoo-mayn) adj.	compassionate, merciful to mankind.	
GYN	**woman**	____________________
gynecology (gi-ne-kol-o-jee) n.	scientific study of female reproductive system and its diseases.	
misogynist (mi-soj-i-nist) n.	person who hates women.	
philogyny (fi-law-gi-nee) n.	love of women.	
gynarchy (gine-ar-kee) n.	government by a woman or women.	
gynecomorphous (gi-nee-ko-mor-fus) adj.	having the form or structural characteristics of a female.	
gyneolatry (gi-nee-ol-atree) n.	excessive fondness or adoration for women.	

REVIEW

Mark the letter of the correct word for each definition in the space provided.

1. **to grow rapidly**
   a. hearken b. burgeon c. gerrymander ________
2. **to be in accordance with rules**
   a. contemplative b. complacent c. conformity ________
3. **irrational fear of thunder and lightning**
   a. chromatography b. ceraunophobia c. paraphobia ________
4. **to sympathize with**
   a. commemorate b. conundrum c. commiserate ________
5. **dislike of mankind in general**
   a. anthropomorphism b. misanthrope c. philanthropy ________
6. **easily angered**
   a. cholera b. choleric c. colic ________
7. **to dig up something buried**
   a. exasperate b. escutcheon c. exhume ________
8. **to come down to the level of another as an equal**
   a. conciliatory b. condescend c. concierge ________
9. **person who hates women**
   a. philogyny b. misogamist c. misogynist ________
10. **not subject to change**
    a. constant b. convoluted c. coherent ________

Mark the letter or write the word that best completes each sentence.

1. The lawyer brought in additional evidence to ____________ his argument.
   a. buttress b. barrister c. barrage
2. The criminal felt a ____________ to murder and was judged insane.
   a. compulsion b. connotation c. conjecture
3. Anyone who has ever been depressed can ____________ moodiness in friends.
   a. confer b. condone c. conscript
4. He doesn't know the answer yet, but he is willing to ____________ on the matter.
   a. cogitate b. coagulate c. collaborate
5. Nations filled with hungry people ____________ for food.
   a. cleave b. castigate c. clamor
6. The couple's new home includes a ____________ living room.
   a. capricious b. capacious c. compensatory
7. Walking down a dark alley makes us tend to be ____________.
   a. charismatic b. chagrin c. chary
8. It takes a good deal of confidence to be ____________ about one's life.
   a. candid b. contiguous c. capillary
9. One must make the choice to be vegetarian or ____________.
   a. carcinogenic b. carnivorous c. copulative
10. Two world wars are responsible for the ____________ of entire cities.
    a. carafe b. carbine c. carnage
11. Knowledge of geography is imperative to ____________.
    a. calligraphy b. cartography c. lexicography
12. To laugh at another person's mistakes is a ____________ act.
    a. churlish b. clairvoyant c. cervical
13. After a number of fights, the boy tried to ____________ with the other.
    a. confiscate b. conjugate c. conciliate

decorous (dek-o-rus)—proper; in good taste; conventional; well-behaved
See **the chorus** of cats **well-behaved**.

22

EXAMPLE OF USE

1. I could give no **credence** to his story, it was so outrageous!
2. The driver of the getaway car is just as **culpable** as the robber.
3. The **cumulative** effects of his economic policy finally plunged the country into a depression.
4. There was a **dearth** of jobs for the applicants after the defense plant layoff.
5. His major **debility** was his bad back.
6. The anniversary marked the end of two **decades** of business.
7. Her **decorous** behavior pleases her mother.
8. The committee decided to **defer** the vote until next week.
9. The worshippers were shocked to see the sacred objects **defiled**.
10. Every summer fire seems to **denude** the hillside.
11. The box of matches burst into sudden flame, **depilating** his eyebrows and hair.
12. The **despot** imposed unreasonable taxes on his subjects.
13. He is equally **dexterous** at writing with either his right or left hand.
14. Her **diaphanous** blouse caused every man in the room to gasp with pleasure.
15. His speech was difficult to follow, as he constantly seemed to **digress** from the main point.
16. She looked upon him with **disdain** when he proposed marriage.
17. While sewing, she made an error that caused her to **disjoin** the sleeve from the bodice and start over.
18. They sent the urgent message with all **dispatch**.
19. No amount of reassurance can **dispel** her fear of enclosed places.
20. One assignment for the biology class was **dissection** of a frog.

The most important element in a human being is his thought. The next is the manner in which he communicates his thought.
—Thomas A. Knott

WORD	DEFINITION	ASSOCIATION *Create and write your associations in the spaces provided!*
1. **credence** (cree-dens) n.	belief; credit	___
2. **culpable** (kul-pa-bel) adj.	blameworthy	___
3. **cumulative** (kyoo-myu-la-tiv) adj.	increasing by successive additions	___
4. **dearth** (durth) n.	extreme scarcity	___
5. **debility** (di-bil-itee) n.	handicap; weakness	___
6. **decade** (dek-ayd) n.	ten years' time	___
7. **decorous** (dek-o-rus) adj.	proper; in good taste; conventional; well-behaved	See **the chorus** of cats **well-behaved**.
8. **defer** (de-fur) v.	delay or postpone	___
9. **defile** (de-fil) v.	make unclean or impure	___
10. **denude** (de-nood) v.	to strip; lay bare	___
11. **depilate** (de-pil-ayt) v.	remove hair from	___
12. **despot** (des-pot) n.	absolute ruler; tyrant	___
13. **dexterous** (dek-strus) adj.	expert; skillful in handling things	___
14. **diaphanous** (di-af-a-nus) adj.	light; delicate; almost transparent	___
15. **digress** (di-gres) v.	deviate from main point	___
16. **disdain** (dis-dayn) n.	contempt; scorn	___
17. **disjoin** (dis-join) v.	to detach; undo; separate	___
18. **dispatch** (di-spach) v.	haste; speed; promptness	___
19. **dispel** (di-spel) v.	dissipate; drive away	___
20. **dissection** (di-sek-shon) n.	separate into parts for analysis	___

bon, ben—good, well

The **bon-bons** are so **good**,
they make me feel **well**.

WORD ROOT	MEANING	ASSOCIATION *Create and write your associations in the spaces provided!*
BON, BEN	**good, well**	The **bon-bons** are so good, they make me feel well!
benefit (ben-e-fit) n.	something helpful and good.	
beneficial (ben-e-fish-al) adj.	having a good or useful effect.	
benefactor ben-e-fak-tor) n.	a person who does good for others.	
benediction (ben-e-dik-shon) n.	a spoken blessing.	
benevolent (be-nev-o-lent) adj.	wishing to do good to others.	
bonanza (bo-nan-za) n.	source of sudden great wealth.	
MAL	**bad, evil**	______________________
maltreated (mal-treet-ed) adj.	treated badly.	
malice (mal-is) n.	desire to harm others.	
malcontent (mal-kon-tent) n.	discontented person inclined to rebel.	
malevolent (ma-lev-o-lent) adj.	wishing evil or harm to others.	
malapropism (mal-a-prop-iz-em) n.	a comical confusion of words.	
malign (ma-lyn) adj.	harmful; showing malice.	
GRAT	**pleasing**	______________________
grateful (grayt-ful) adj.	showing one values a kindness received.	
gratuity (gra-too-i-tee) n.	money given for services rendered.	
congratulation (kon-grach-u-lay-shon) n.	show pleasure through praise.	
ingratiate (in-gray-shi-ayt) v.	bring oneself into a person's favor.	
gratitude (grat-i-tood) n.	being grateful.	
ingrate (in-grayt) n.	person who is not grateful.	

REVIEW

Draw a line between the word and its correct definition.

1. **dispel**	a. increasing successively
2. **disjoin**	b. belief
3. **dexterous**	c. handicap
4. **decorous**	d. to lay bare
5. **denude**	e. skillful in handling something
6. **decade**	f. to deviate from the main point
7. **debility**	g. ten years' time
8. **cumulative**	h. to drive away
9. **credence**	i. contempt
10. **defer**	j. to detach
11. **digress**	k. proper
12. **disdain**	l. to delay
13. **dispatch**	m. to send off a message

Circle the correct word below each definition.

1. **scarcity**
   (scaphoid, debacle, dearth, decathlon)
2. **a person who does good for others**
   (beneficiary, bidentate, benefactor, blackguard)
3. **to make impure**
   (designate, decimate, demarcate, defile)
4. **tyrant**
   (despot, snafu, avant-garde, avatar)
5. **to separate into parts for analysis**
   (dissipation, dissection, disparage, disfigure)
6. **to be responsible for a misdeed**
   (culinary, culpable, croissant, convulsive)
7. **almost transparent**
   (diabolical, diatribe, diaphanous, dilapidated)
8. **person who is not grateful**
   (grouse, ingrate, inveterate, surrogate)
9. **to remove hair from**
   (depurate, denunciate, depilate, decimate)
10. **a comical confusion of words**
    (malignant, malleate, malapropism, malediction)

doff (dof)—take off clothing; put aside 23
He said, "take **it doff**, and **put** it **aside**."

EXAMPLE OF USE

1. His parole officer tried to **dissuade** him from contacting his old friends.

2. During our debate, my opponent tried to **distort** everything I said.

3. After the sudden downpour, she **divested** herself of the wet clothes.

4. The hot sun prompted me to **doff** my coat.

5. The **dolt** couldn't seem to follow the simplest instructions.

6. He amused his students with his **droll** lectures.

7. Because she was so vain, she was easily **duped** by his flattery.

8. An **ectomorph** is characteristically lean and slightly muscular.

9. The king's tax **edict** prompted an uprising among the people.

10. He tried to **efface** the memory of the automobile accident.

11. We admired the beautiful gowns the ladies were wearing as they **egressed** from the theater.

12. The professor was asked to **elucidate** his theory of economics.

13. Flames began to **emanate** from the burning building.

14. The **embargo** on oil from the Middle East depleted domestic supplies.

15. He had planned for years to **emigrate** to the United States from Europe; permission was finally granted, and he leaves today.

16. I felt **empathy** for the stage performer when he continually missed his cues.

17. It is estimated that in two hours the town will be **engulfed** by the flood waters.

18. The salesman was told to **enumerate** his expenses on his report.

19. Listening to his description, I began to **envisage** the Mona Lisa in its place in the Louvre.

20. The two men began to hurl angry **epithets** at each other across the table.

Words are the best medium of exchange of thoughts and ideas between people.
—William Ross

WORD	DEFINITION	ASSOCIATION *Create and write your associations in the spaces provided!*
1. **dissuade** (di-swayd) v.	advise or persuade against	________
2. **distort** (di-stort) v.	to twist; render untrue	________
3. **divest** (di-vest) v.	undress; deprive; dispossess	________
4. **doff** (dof) v.	take off clothing; put aside	He said, "**take it doff**, and put it **aside**."
5. **dolt** (dohlt) n.	dull or stupid person	________
6. **droll** (drohl) adj.	amusing; comic; odd	________
7. **dupe** (doop) n.	a person easily tricked	________
8. **ectomorph** (ek-to-morf) n.	individual with light body build	________
9. **edict** (ee-dikt) n.	public command by leader having the force of law	________
10. **efface** (eh-fays) v.	erase; obliterate; make inconspicuous	________
11. **egress** (ee-gres) n.	exit; act of going out	________
12. **elucidate** (i-loo-si-dayt) v.	explain; illustrate; make clear	________
13. **emanate** (em-a-nayt) v.	emit; flow out or issue from a source	________
14. **embargo** (em-bahr-goh) n.	prohibition; restraint	________
15. **emigrate** (em-i-grayt) v.	leave one country or region to settle in another	________
16. **empathy** (em-pa-thee) n.	capacity for understanding another's feelings	________
17. **engulf** (en-gulf) v.	swallow up; overwhelm	________
18. **enumerate** (i-noo-me-rayt) v.	to count; number; list	________
19. **envisage** (en-viz-ij) v.	form a mental picture; imagine; foresee	________
20. **epithet** (ep-i-that) n.	descriptive word or phrase	________

arch—ruler, govern

See the **ruler,** holding his **ruler** sitting on the **arch governing** away.

WORD ROOT	MEANING	ASSOCIATION *Create and write your associations in the spaces provided!*
ARCH	**ruler, govern**	See the **ruler**, holding his **ruler**, sitting on the **arch governing** away.
anarchy (an-ar-kee) n.	absence of government or control.	
monarch (mon-ark) n.	a ruler with title of king, emperor, etc.	
hierarchy (hi-e-rahr-kee) n.	a group of persons or things arranged in order of rank, status or class.	
architect (ahr-ki-tekt) n.	a person who designs a building.	
matriarch (may-tri-ahrk) n.	a woman as head of a tribe or family.	
oligarchy (ol-i-gahr-kee) n.	a country governed by a few people.	
DUC, DUCE, DUCT	**lead**	______________________
educate ej-u-kayt) v.	to train the minds and skills of.	
seduce (si-doos) v.	to persuade by offering temptations.	
induce (in-doos) v.	to persuade by inductive reasoning.	
introduction (in-tro-duk-shon) n.	formal presentation of one person to another.	
deduct (di-dukt) v.	to take away an amount or quantity.	
abduct (ab-dukt) v.	to carry off a person by force or fraud.	
FEDER, FID	**trust, faith**	______________________
federal (fed-e-ral) adj.	system of government—states united under central authority but remain independent in internal affairs	
confederacy (kon-fed-e-ra-see) n.	a union of people or states by treaty.	
confide (kon-fyd) v.	to entrust information confidentially.	
infidel (in-fi-del) n.	a person with no religious beliefs.	
bona fide (boh-na-fyd) adj.	genuine, without fraud.	
perfidy (pur-fi-dee) n.	disloyal, treacherous.	

REVIEW

Mark true or false in the space provided.

1. ________ An **epithet** is an inscription on a tombstone.
2. ________ An **ectomorph** is someone with a slight body size.
3. ________ **Anarchy** is a system of people organized by rank.
4. ________ A **dolt** is a young donkey.
5. ________ To **emigrate** is to leave the country.
6. ________ An **embargo** is a unique ship for carrying cargo.
7. ________ **Perfidy** is the tendency toward perfectionism.
8. ________ To **elucidate** a problem is to explain it clearly.
9. ________ To **enumerate** a list of faults is to count them.
10. ________ An **edict** is a small, oblong pastry.

Mark the letter from column 2 that best describes each word in column 1.

1		2
envisage	________	a. persuade against some action
engulf	________	b. to put aside
empathy	________	c. to twist information
egress	________	d. a person easily tricked
doff	________	e. to overwhelm
droll	________	f. to make inconspicuous
dissuade	________	g. to issue from a source
divest	________	h. to deprive
dupe	________	i. to exit
emanate	________	j. form a mental picture
abduct	________	k. oddly amusing
distort	________	l. capacity for understanding others
efface	________	m. to carry off by force

24

facade (fa-sahd)—front part of building

See the **face** painted on the **front part of the building**.

EXAMPLE OF USE

1. He disputed the **equity** of the system of grading on the curve.

2. "To **err** is human, to forgive divine."

3. When the **etiology** of cancer is known, then a cure can be found.

4. The Oxford English Dictionary traces each word's **etymology**.

5. The Nazis endorsed **eugenics** as a means of producing a "pure Aryan race."

6. The poet was taken with the **euphonious** combination of words he had written.

7. The pleasures of youth are **evanescent**.

8. Many Russian ballet dancers have **expatriated** to the United States.

9. The clerk was asked to **expedite** the processing of the invoice.

10. The young lady's mother was always quick to **extol** her daughter's many virtues.

11. The writer's prose would read so much better without all those **extraneous** words.

12. Judging from the **facade**, that building was designed in the 1920s.

13. Although her parents took his outrageous remarks seriously, she knew he was being **facetious**.

14. It was a struggle to show even a **factitious** interest in that dull subject.

15. He was not taken in by his friend's **fallacious** reasoning.

16. After paying to hear him lecture, we were annoyed by his **fatuous** comments.

17. The biology class studied local **fauna** and flora.

18. His religious **fervor** was apparent to everyone who knew him.

19. The **fetid** sewer annoyed eveyone in the neighborhood.

20. Black stockings are his **fetish**.

The righteous need no tombstones; their words are their monument.
—Talmud: Pasahim 119a

WORD	DEFINITION	ASSOCIATION *Create and write your associations in the spaces provided!*
1. **equity** (ek-wi-tee) n.	that which is equally right or just to all concerned	__________
2. **err** (ur) v.	make a mistake	__________
3. **etiology** (ee-ti-ol-o-jee) n.	science of origins and causes, especially of disease	__________
4. **etymology** (et-i-mol-o-jee) n.	study of origin of words & their meanings	__________
5. **eugenics** (yoo-jen-iks) n.	science of generative improvement of human race	__________
6. **euphonious** (yoo-foh-ni-us) adj.	pleasing to the ear	__________
7. **evanescent** (ev-a-nes-ent) adj.	vanishing; fleeting; fading quickly	__________
8. **expatriate** (eks-pay-tri-it) n.	one who is exiled or who withdraws his citizenship	__________
9. **expedite** (ek-spe-dite) v.	hasten; accelerate motion of; perform quickly	__________
10. **extol** (ik-stohl) v.	praise highly; eulogize	__________
11. **extraneous** (ik-stray-ni-us) adj.	outside; unrelated; not essential to subject	__________
12. **facade** (fa-sahd) n.	front part of building	See the **face** painted on the **front part of the building**.
13. **facetious** (fa-see-shus) adj.	playful; joking; intending to be amusing	__________
14. **factitious** (fak-tish-us) adj.	artificial; unnatural	__________
15. **fallacious** (fa-lay-shus) adj.	falsely believed; misleading	__________
16. **fatuous** (fach-oo-us) adj.	conceited; foolish; silly	__________
17. **fauna** (faw-na) n.	animal life of area or period of time	__________
18. **fervor** (fur-vor) n.	passion; warmth of feeling; zeal	__________
19. **fetid** (fet-id) adj.	stinking; having offensive smell	__________
20. **fetish** (fet-ish) n.	object of blind devotion, often sexual	__________

gam—marriage

Marriage is a **gambling game**.

WORD ROOT	MEANING	ASSOCIATION *Create and write your associations in the spaces provided!*
GAM	**marriage**	**Marriage** is a **gambling game.**
monogamy (mo-nog-a-mee) n.	system of marriage to only one person at a time.	
bigamy (big-a-mee) n.	marriage to two people at one time.	
polygamy (po-lig-a-mee) n.	system of marriage to more than one person.	
misogamist (mi-sog-a-mist) n.	a person who hates marriage.	
gamete (gam-eet) n.	a sexual cell capable of fusing with another in reproduction.	
gamogenesis (gam-o-gin-e-sis) n.	reproduction by the uniting of gametes.	
PATR, PATER	**father**	______________________
patriotism (pay-tri-o-tiz-em) n.	loyalty to one's country.	
expatriate (eks-pay-tri-it) n.	person leaving one's native country to live abroad.	
patriarch (pay-tri-ark) n.	male head of a family or tribe.	
patricide (pat-ri-syd) n.	act of killing one's father.	
patronize (pay-tro-niz) v.	to support or encourage an activity or cause.	
paternal (pa-tur-nal) adj.	acting as a father.	
MATR, MATER	**mother**	______________________
matrimony (mat-ri-moh-nee) n.	marriage.	
maternity (ma-tur-ni-tee) n.	motherhood.	
matricide (mat-ri-syd) n.	act of killing one's mother.	
matriarch (may-tri-ahrk) n.	woman who is head of family or tribe.	
matriculation (ma-trik-yu-lay-shon) n.	enrolled as a student in a college or university.	
matron (may-tron) n.	a married woman.	

REVIEW

Mark the letter of the correct word for each definition in the space provided.

1. **the front part of a building**
   a. facile b. facade c. farthing ________
2. **marriage to more than one person**
   a. polymorphism b. polyglot c. polygamy ________
3. **the act of killing one's mother**
   a. maternity b. matricide c. matriculation ________
4. **the science of improving the human race**
   a. euphorbia b. euphemism c. eugenics ________
5. **a person who doesn't live in his own country**
   a. epicure b. executrix c. expatriate ________
6. **artificial**
   a. vacuous b. factitious c. facetious ________
7. **the study of words and their meanings**
   a. etiology b. etymology c. seismology ________
8. **fading quickly**
   a. evangelical b. evocative c. evanescent ________
9. **the science of origins and causes**
   a. ethnology b. sociology c. etiology ________
10. **pleasing to the ear**
    a. symphonic b. phonetic c. euphonic ________

Mark the letter or write the word that best completes each sentence.

1. The U.S. Constitution is designed to achieve ____________ among all people.
   a. pederasty b. disparity c. equity
2. To ____________ in human affairs is a fact of life.
   a. germinate b. err c. ferret
3. To ____________ matters, he solved the problem on his own.
   a. evade b. expedite c. exemplify
4. The national parks are famous for flora and ____________.
   a. daemon b. feces c. fauna
5. The valedictorian delivered his speech with genuine ____________.
   a. fervor b. halcyon c. lactose
6. Having a shoe ____________ is a matter of grave concern.
   a. filature b. fetish c. facet
7. After several hours on the stove, the eggs had left a ____________ odor.
   a. facile b. febrile c. fetid
8. The ____________ storyteller talked for hours and bored everyone.
   a. factional b. filibuster c. fatuous
9. To believe the words of any politician these days is ____________ thinking.
   a. fluorescent b. fallacious c. fandango
10. When great men die, even their critics ____________ their virtues.
    a. excrete b. extol c. exacerbate
11. People who observe decorum demonstrate the ____________ times we live in.
    a. exponential b. follicular c. factitious
12. Don't be ____________; it's an absurd idea.
    a. fractious b. facetious c. flatulent
13. It is not useful to study information that is ____________ to the subject.
    a. extracurricular b. inextricable c. extraneous

25

frigid (frij-id)—cold; icy; coldly; formal; lifeless

See the **formal**-looking penguin keeping cool in the **icy cold fridge**.

EXAMPLE OF USE

1. To protect themselves against lawsuits, many writers declare that the people and incidents they write about are purely **fictitious.**
2. Although she believed it had really happened, the incident proved to be a **figment** of her imagination.
3. The earthquake caused a **fissure** in the main street of town.
4. I can tell that these vegetables aren't fresh because they are **flaccid**, not firm.
5. On ancient sailing ships, it was thought that **flagellation** of the slaves would make them row faster.
6. She had to **forgo** breakfast in order to get to class on time.
7. His **fortuitous** arrival saved me from walking to the gas station.
8. She tends to be **fractious,** so don't contradict her unless you're prepared for an argument.
9. I was uncomfortable in the **frigid** climate of Alaska, but the Eskimoes were accustomed to it.
10. The concessions he made were part of a **gambit** calculated to give him an edge in the negotiations.
11. She hoped to **garner** enough goodwill from her colleagues to be appointed chairman.
12. Her hobby is tracing her family's **genealogy**.
13. The power plant began to **generate** electricity.
14. Researchers in the field of **genetics** believe that many diseases are caused by heredity.
15. The Nazis practiced **genocide** against the Jews during World War II.
16. Because he was born a member of the landed **gentry**, he led a life of privilege.
17. The company drilled for oil based upon the **geologist's** report.
18. When the speaker became overly emotional, he **gesticulated** wildly.
19. The **gist** of the letter had to do with legal matters, even though some family news was mixed in.
20. The family came away from the burial feeling very **glum**.

Alice had not the slightest idea what Latitude was, or Longitude either, but she thought they were nice grand words to say. —Lewis Carroll, *Alice's Adventures in Wonderland*, ch. 1

WORD	DEFINITION	ASSOCIATION *Create and write your associations in the spaces provided!*
1. **fictitious** (fik-tish-us) adj.	not real; existing in the imagination	______
2. **figment** (fig-ment) n.	something imagined; an invention of the mind	______
3. **fissure** (fish-ur) n.	cleft made by splitting or separation of parts	______
4. **flaccid** (flak-sid) adj.	slack; droopy; flabby; not firm	______
5. **flagellate** (flaj-e-layt) v.	to whip or lash; punish	______
6. **forgo** (for-goh) v.	pass by without claiming; give up	______
7. **fortuitous** (for-too-i-tus) adj.	accidental; happening by chance	______
8. **fractious** (frak-shus) adj.	apt to quarrel; peevish	______
9. **frigid** (frij-id) adj.	cold; icy; coldly formal; lifeless	See for **formal**-looking penguin keeping cool in the **icy cold fridge**.
10. **gambit** (gam-bit) n.	calculated move intended to secure some advantage	______
11. **garner** (gahr-ner) v.	accumulate; earn	______
12. **genealogy** (jee-ni-ol-o-jee) n.	history of family descent; lineage	______
13. **generate** (jen-e-rayt) v.	produce; cause; bring into existence	______
14. **genetics** (je-net-iks) adj.	study of genes, heredity	______
15. **genocide** (gen-o-side) n.	deliberate killing of a particular race or group	______
16. **gentry** (jen-tree) n.	class of well-born and well-bred people; aristocracy	______
17. **geologist** (jee-ol-o-jist) n.	one who studies rocks and structure of Earth's crust	______
18. **gesticulate** (je-stik-yu-layt) v.	make gestures, esp. of hands and arms	______
19. **gist** (jist) n.	main point	______
20. **glum** (glum) adj.	gloomily sullen; moody; frowning	______

ex—out

See him **'X'ing out** the words by the **exit** sign.

WORD ROOT	MEANING	ASSOCIATION *Create and write your associations in the spaces provided!*
EX	**out**	See him **'X'ing out** the words by the **exit** sign.
excitable (ik-sy-ta-bel) adj.	feeling strongly.	
exclaim (ik-sklaym) v.	to cry out suddenly from pain or pleasure.	
exit (ek-sit) v.	the act of going out or away.	
expect (ik-spekt) v.	to think or believe that a thing will happen.	
expelled (ik-speld) v.	to force out.	
exception (ik-sep-shon) n.	thing that does not follow general rule.	
E, EC, EF	**out**	______________________________
effete (i-feet) adj.	having lost its vitality.	
ecstasy (ek-sta-see) n.	a feeling of intense delight.	
effervescent (ef-er-ves-ent) adj.	giving off small bubbles of gas.	
effect (i-fekt) n.	change produced by a cause or an action.	
effort (ef-ort) n.	use of energy to achieve something.	
eccentric (ik-sen-trik) adj.	unconventional in appearance or behavior.	
DE	**away, from**	______________________________
defend (di-fend) v.	protect by warding off an attack.	
deprive (di-pryv) v.	to take a thing away from.	
deformed (di-formd) adj.	put out of shape.	
delude (di-lood) v.	to deceive or trick someone.	
decadence (dek-a-dens) n.	less worthy in standards.	
deride (di-ryd) v.	to laugh at scornfully.	

REVIEW

Draw a line between the word and its correct definition.

1. **gambit**	a. make gestures
2. **generate**	b. history of a family
3. **glum**	b. apt to quarrel
4. **expelled**	d. main point
5. **delude**	e. calculated move
6. **genealogy**	f. to force out
7. **fractious**	g. unconventional
8. **eccentric**	h. to deceive
9. **gesticulate**	i. bring into existence
10. **gist**	j. moody

Circle the correct word below each definition.

1. **existing in the imagination**
   (fragmentary, fictitious, fortuitous, fetishistic)
2. **cold and lifeless**
   (fecund, frigid, febrile, farcical)
3. **one who studies the structure of the Earth's crust**
   (geophysicist, geometrician, geologist, geographer)
4. **flabby**
   (flotsam, flaccid, funicular, fuminant)
5. **cleft made by splitting**
   (fissure, filibuster, filament, fauces)
6. **something imagined**
   (fibula, figment, fallacy, facsimile)
7. **the study of heredity**
   (genitalia, genealogy, genetics, geopolitics)
8. **pass by without claiming**
   (forage, forgo, forebode, foment)
9. **happening by chance**
   (forensic, foregone, fortuitous, forlorn)
10. **to punish with a whip**
    (fluctuate, flagellate, flocculate, fleece)
11. **to store up**
    (garnish, gamble, garner, galvanize)
12. **group of people born into a high class**
    (serfs, gentile, gentry, gerontocracy)
13. **deliberate destruction of a particular race of humans**
    (geriatrics, genocide, gossamer, grotesquerie)

grovel (gruv-el)—to crawl in fear or humility; to humble oneself
See a person **groveling** in the **gravel**.

26

EXAMPLE OF USE

1. The pulverized glass was **granular** like sand.
2. Although some people think it's ridiculous, some firms use **graphology** to pinpoint character flaws in potential employees.
3. The union shop formed a committee to air employees' **grievances** against management.
4. When the football player was hurt, he **grimaced** in pain.
5. The executive has no respect for a "yes-man" who **grovels** at his feet.
6. Once you saw beyond his **gruff** exterior, you could see that he was a nice man.
7. Every woman should have her **gynecologist** test her once a year for cervical cancer.
8. The judge issued a writ of **habeas corpus** in order to hear the accused and decide whether or not to release him.
9. The **hapless** man has become a bum sleeping in doorways on Skid Row.
10. She began to **harangue** him about mowing the lawn.
11. He put his feet up on the **hassock** and leaned back in the chair to watch television.
12. That man is such a **hedonist**—all he thinks about is his own pleasure.
13. **Hematology** is one of the most important tools a doctor has to diagnose disorders that show up in the blood.
14. Don't try feeding that giraffe any meat; he is an **herbivorous** animal.
15. The building of the pyramids was a **herculean** task.
16. A zoo's house of **herpetology** contains many varieties of snakes.
17. The **hierarchy** of the Catholic clergy is arranged with the Pope at the top, followed by the cardinals, bishops, priests, etc.
18. The man was arrested and charged with **homicide**.
19. It was just another **humdrum** dinner party at Sue's house.
20. His prize-winning **hybrid** rose was a cross between two well-known varieties.

Words are the tools we build our knowledge with.
—Scott Bornstein

WORD	DEFINITION	ASSOCIATION *Create and write your associations in the spaces provided!*
1. **granular** (gran-yu-lar) adj.	composed of or resembling grains or granules	
2. **graphology** (gra-fol-o-jee) n.	study of handwriting as expression of character	
3. **grievance** (gree-vans) n.	cause of grief; distress; hardship	
4. **grimace** (grim-as) n.	distortion of face expressing pain, disgust	
5. **grovel** (gruv-el) v.	to crawl in fear or humility; to humble oneself	See a person **groveling** in the **gravel**.
6. **gruff** (gruf) adj.	rough or stern in manner; surly; hoarse	
7. **gynecologist** (gi-ne-kol-o-jist) n.	doctor specializing in the study of female reproduction	
8. **habeas corpus** (hay-bi-as kor-pus) n.	legal writ requiring one's appearance before a judge	
9. **hapless** (hap-lis) adj.	unlucky; ill-fated	
10. **harangue** (ha-rang) n.	tirade; argue about; lengthy, bombastic speech	
11. **hassock** (has-ok) n.	large cushion used as a footrest	
12. **hedonist** (hee-do-nist) n.	one who regards pleasure as chief good in life	
13. **hematology** (hee-ma-tol-o-jee) n.	branch of biology relating to study of blood	
14. **herbivorous** (hur-biv-o-rus) adj.	feeding on vegetation	
15. **herculean** (hur-kyu-lee-an) adj.	tremendous in size, courage; as strong as Hercules	
16. **herpetology** (hur-pe-tol-o-jee) n.	science of reptiles & amphibians	
17. **hierarchy** (hi-e-rahr-kee) n.	group, officials, or terms organized by rank	
18. **homicide** (hom-i-side) n.	murder; killing of one human by another	
19. **humdrum** (hum-drum) adj.	monotony; tediousness; routine	
20. **hybrid** (hi-brid) n.	crossbreed; offspring of different species	

con, com, coh—with, together

See the **cons** all **together coming with** the jail keeper.

WORD ROOT	MEANING	ASSOCIATION *Create and write your associations in the spaces provided!*
CON, COM, COH	**with, together**	See the **cons** all **together coming with** the jail-keeper
connect (ko-nekt) v.	to join or be joined.	
congregate (kon-gre-gayt) v.	flock together into a crowd.	
congress (kong-gris) n.	formal meeting of representatives for discussion.	
combine (kom-byn) v.	to join into a group or set.	
compound (kom-pownd) adj.	made up of several parts.	
cohere (koh-heer) v.	to stick together.	
INTRO	**within**	______________________
intrastate (in-tra-stayt) adj.	within a state.	
intravenous (in-tra-vee-nus) adj.	in, into or within a vein.	
intradepartmental (in-tra-de-part-ment-al) adj.	within the department.	
intraneural (in-tra-nyur-al) adj.	within the nerve.	
intrabred (in-tra-bred) adj.	matings within tribe or race.	
intracontinental (in-tra-kon-ti-nen-tal) adj.	within the continent.	
LESS	**without**	______________________
homeless (hohm-lis) adj.	without a place to live.	
effortless (ef-ort-lis) adj.	done without effort.	
weightless (wayt-lis) adj.	without weight.	
powerless (pow-er-lis) adj.	without power to take action.	
fearless (feer-lis) adj.	feeling no fear.	
careless (kair-lis) adj.	not careful.	

REVIEW

Mark true or false in the space provided.

1. ________ A **hedonist** is always concerned with living by morals.
2. ________ A **hybrid** is the offspring of two different species.
3. ________ To **grovel** is to dig for remnants of ancient civilizations.
4. ________ A **habeas corpus** is a legal writ requiring a court appearance.
5. ________ A **hassock** is a Russian peasant.
6. ________ **Hematology** is the study of blood.
7. ________ An **intravenous** injection goes into the veins.
8. ________ A **grimace** is a troll as in a fable.
9. ________ A **compound** is made up of several parts.
10. ________ **Herpetology** is the study of vaginal diseases.

Mark the letter from column 2 that best describes each word in column 1.

1		2
granular	________	a. monotonous
hapless	________	b. tremendous strength
humdrum	________	c. a lengthy argument
herculean	________	d. stern manner
herbivorous	________	e. complaint about hardships
harangue	________	f. a group organized by rank
grievance	________	g. unlucky
gynecologist	________	h. murder
graphology	________	i. study of handwriting for character analysis
gruff	________	j. doctor specializing in female reproduction
hierarchy	________	k. done with ease
homicide	________	l. resembling grains
effortless	________	m. feeding on vegetation

27

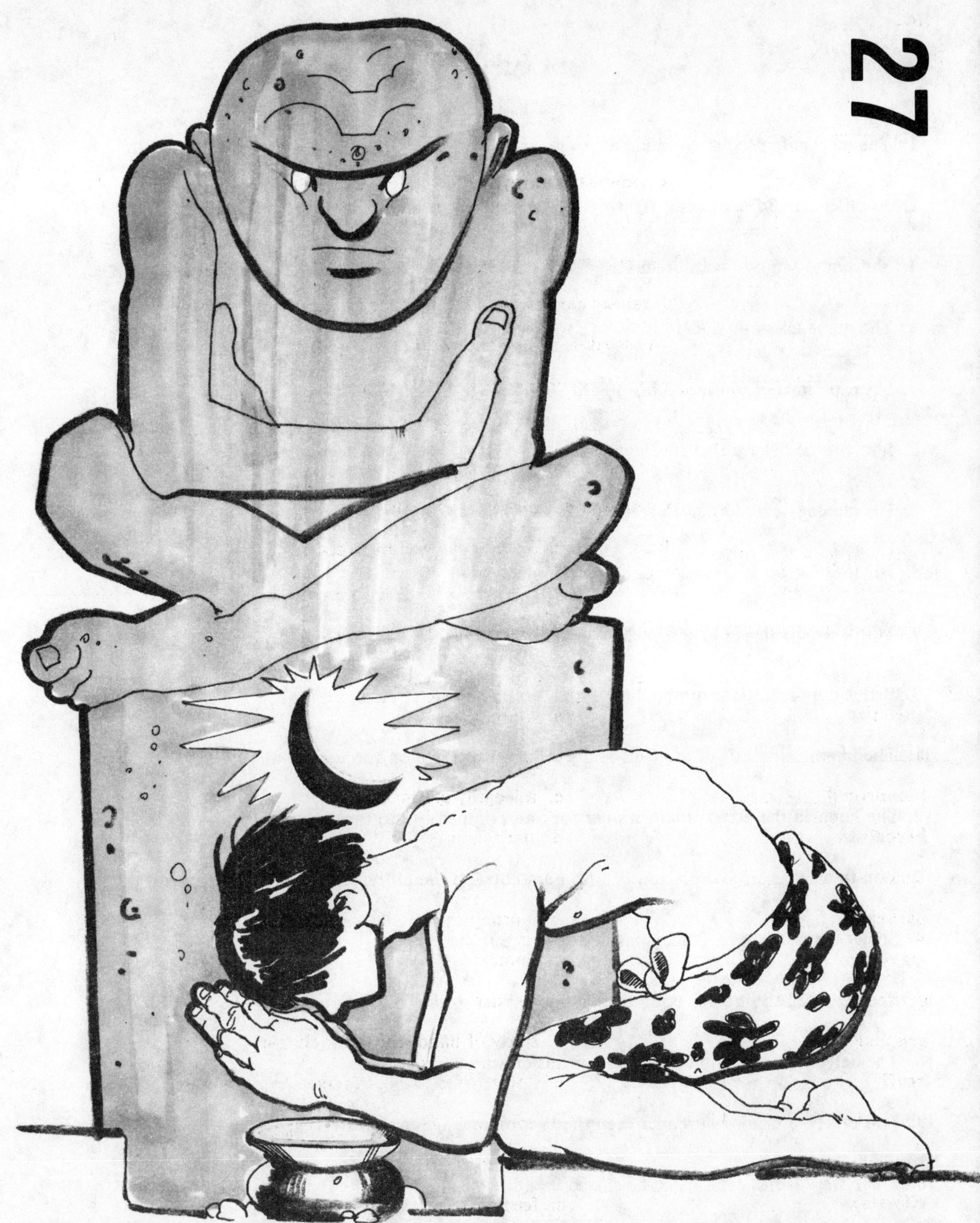

idolatry (i-dol-a-tree)—worship of created objects; blind devotion
See someone **worshipping** the **idol**.

EXAMPLE OF USE

1. The mechanic used a **hydraulic** lift to raise the car.
2. Another name for rabies is **hydrophobia,** because of the disease's final symptoms.
3. She cannot enjoy opera because she is **hypersensitive** to the high-pitched notes.
4. The nurse uses a **hypodermic** syringe to inject the medication.
5. His experiments confirmed his original **hypothesis**.
6. It's hard to believe that this **iconoclast** used to be a staunch defender of all that he now reviles.
7. His **ideology** caused him to reject much of what our society values.
8. His love for art objects comes close to **idolatry**.
9. This is an **idyllic** spot for a picnic.
10. Better opportunities prompted the family to **immigrate** to Australia.
11. The **immortal** words of the Gettysburg Address will live on forever.
12. She **impaled** the bread cube with her fork and dipped it into the cheese fondue.
13. You think you are correct and I think I am correct; therefore, we are at an **impasse**.
14. Soviet **imperialism** has encompassed Eastern Europe.
15. She hesitated to **impinge** upon their friendship by asking for such a big favor.
16. The defective flask **imploded** as the air inside was suctioned out.
17. Too much to drink can render even the best raconteur **inarticulate**.
18. There were ladies present, so he cursed **inaudibly**.
19. A broken leg **incapacitated** her for six weeks.
20. The baby's **incessant** crying made her parents frantic.

He knew the precise psychological moment when to say nothing.
—Oscar Wilde

WORD	DEFINITION	ASSOCIATION *Create and write your associations in the spaces provided!*
1. **hydraulic** (hi-draw-lik) adj.	operated by means of water or liquid	______________________
2. **hydrophobia** (hi-dro-foh-bi-a) n.	fear of water	______________________
3. **hypersensitive** (hi-per-sen-si-tiv) adj.	excessively sensitive	______________________
4. **hypodermic** (hi-po-dur-mik) adj.	hypo—under; derm—skin: injected under the skin	______________________
5. **hypothesis** (hi-poth-e-sis) n.	tentative assumption	______________________
6. **iconoclast** (i-kon-o-klast) n.	destroyer of customs or cherished belief	______________________
7. **ideology** (i-di-ol-o-jee) n.	set of beliefs characterizing a particular group	______________________
8. **idolatry** (i-dol-a-tree)	worship of created objects; a blind devotion	See someone **worshiping** the **idol**.
9. **idyllic** (i-dil-ik) adj.	peaceful; rustic; rural; happy	______________________
10. **immigrate** (im-i-grayt) v.	move to a new country or location	______________________
11. **immortal** (i-mor-tal) adj.	everlasting; unceasing; living forever	______________________
12. **impale** (im-payl) v.	to thrust a sharpened stake through	______________________
13. **impasse** (im-pas) n.	dead end; deadlock	______________________
14. **imperialism** (im-peer-i-a-liz-em) n.	country's policy to increase its dominion	______________________
15. **impinge** (im-pinj) v.	infringe; intrude or encroach upon	______________________
16. **implosion** (im-ploh-zhon) n.	sudden collapse inward	______________________
17. **inarticulate** (in-ahr-tik-yu-lit) adj.	incapable of distinct speech; unable to express ideas	______________________
18. **inaudible** (in-aw-di-bel) adj.	incapable of being heard	______________________
19. **incapacitate** (in-ka-pas-i-tayt) v.	to render unfit or helpless; to make ineligible	______________________
20. **incessant** (in-ses-ant) adj.	unceasing; continuously repeated	______________________

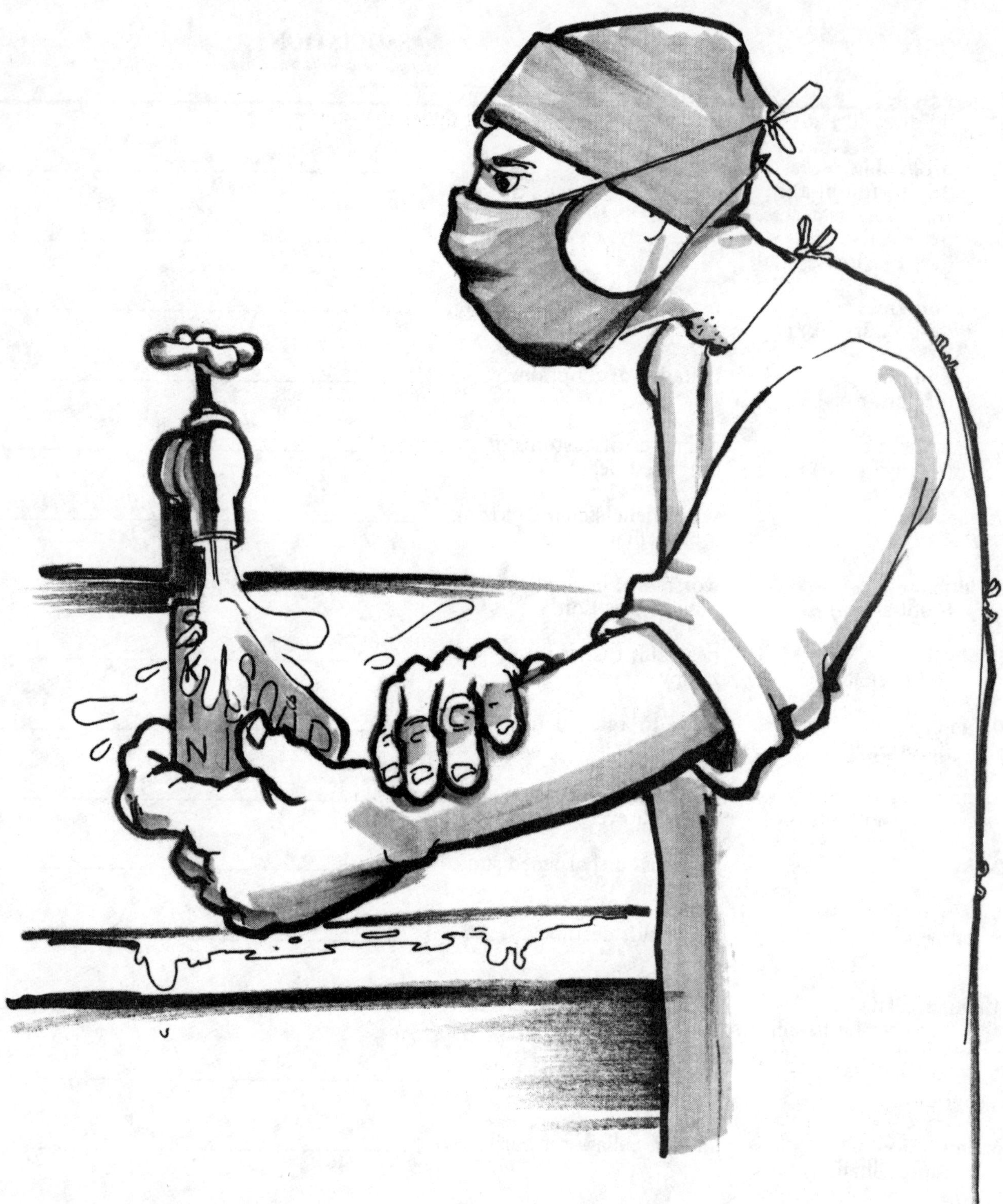

derm—skin

See the doctor washing the **germs** off his **skin**.

WORD ROOT	MEANING	ASSOCIATION *Create and write your associations in the spaces provided!*
DERM	**skin**	See the doctor washing the **germs** off his **skin.**
hypodermic (hi-po-dur-mik) n.	needle for injecting liquid under the skin.	
pachyderm (pak-i-durm) n.	thick-skinned animal.	
dermatologist (dur-me-tol-o-jist) n.	specialist in skin disorders.	
dermatitis (dur-ma-ti-tis) n.	inflammation of the skin.	
epidermis (ep-i-dur-mis) n.	outer layer of the skin.	
dermis (dur-mis) n.	skin, the layer of tissue below the outer layer.	
NEUR	**nerve**	______________________
neurotic (nuu-rot-ik) adj.	subject to abnormal anxieties.	
neurosis (nuu-roh-sis) n.	disorder producing depression or abnormal behavior.	
neural (noor-al) adj.	of nerves.	
neuritis (nuu-ri-tis) n.	inflammation of the nerves.	
neurology (nuu-rol-o-jee) n.	scientific study of nerve systems.	
neurography (nuu-rog-ra-fee) n.	a description of the nervous system.	
OSS, OSTEO	**bone**	______________________
osteopathy (os-ti-op-a-thee) n.	manipulation of bones and muscles.	
ossification (os-i-fi-kay-shon) n.	changed into bone.	
osteodentine (os-te-o-den-teen) n.	bone found in the teeth of fishes.	
osteometry (os-te-om-e-tree) n.	the measuring of bones.	
osteitis (os-tee-ite-is) n.	inflammation of the bone.	
osseous (os-e-us) adj.	bony.	

REVIEW

Mark the letter of the correct word for each definition in the space provided.

1. **blind devotion**
   a. reclusivity b. iconoclast c. idolatry ______
2. **national policy to dominate world affairs**
   a. nepotism b. despotism c. imperialism ______
3. **fear of water**
   a. acrophobia b. hydrophobia c. claustrophobia ______
4. **sudden collapse inward**
   a. explosion b. libation c. implosion ______
5. **thick-skinned animal**
   a. epidermis b. elephantiasis c. pachyderm ______
6. **subject to abnormal anxieties**
   a. pathetic b. neurotic c. lethargic ______
7. **bony**
   a. borosilicate b. osseous c. dystrophy ______
8. **injected under the skin**
   a. hypodermic b. dysmenorrhea c. irredenta ______
9. **to intrude upon**
   a. impel b. instigate c. impinge ______
10. **to come into a new country**
    a. epiphany b. immigrate c. manipulate ______

Mark the letter or write the word that best completes each sentence.

1. The poem from the Romantic era depicts a woman of ___________ beauty.
   a. idyllic b. intrepid c. innocuous
2. Let us consider the ___________ words of Abraham Lincoln.
   a. illicit b. immortal c. impertinent
3. The candidate running for office does not represent any single ___________.
   a. implement b. impresario c. ideology
4. If only the neighbors would stop that ___________ hammering.
   a. impermeable b. ineluctable c. incessant
5. Any leader of a revolution must be an ___________.
   a. idiosyncrasy b. iconoclast c. idol
6. A ___________ must be documented with evidence before it becomes an accepted theory.
   a. hypochondriac b. hypertrophy c. hypothesis
7. She was so weary that she was no longer ___________ in conversation.
   a. acquiescent b. articulate c. altruistic
8. Delegates to the international peace conference reached an ___________.
   a. impasse b. exogamy c. ophthalmia
9. To leave a cripple without a wheelchair will ___________ him.
   a. incarcerate b. incapacitate c. invigorate
10. The cartons were transported to higher shelves by means of a ___________ lift.
    a. hydrophobic b. hydraulic c. hydrofoil
11. The only way to kill a vampire is to ___________ him through the heart.
    a. innoculate b. inseminate c. impale
12. People who worry about everything are ___________.
    a. homologous b. hypersensitive c. hermaphroditic
13. The congressman's remarks were ___________ without a microphone.
    a. inadvertent b. inaudible c. indissoluble

28

ingenious (in-jeen-yus)—marked by inventive genius; cleverly contrived
Picture: the **mark** of a **genius** will be his **clever** ideas.

EXAMPLE OF USE

1. Her father tried to nip the **incipient** romance in the bud.

2. The fares are in effect Monday through Thursday **inclusive**.

3. Because this was the teenager's twelfth arrest, the judge found him to be **incorrigible**.

4. Corn is **indigenous** to the United States.

5. Hot weather in summer makes many of us **indolent**.

6. The rest of the family will **indubitably** contest the old man's will.

7. She is a hopelessly **inept** typist.

8. This is the third time that **infernal** car has broken down in two weeks!

9. Most large metropolitan areas have an enormous **influx** of people hoping to improve their lot in life.

10. You are **infringing** on my privacy when you ask personal questions.

11. The telephone is an **ingenious** device that has vastly improved communications.

12. She had always seemed so sophisticated that we were surprised by her **ingenuous** answers to the Kinsey Report questionnaire.

13. **Ingesting** food is a glutton's favorite pastime.

14. The **inimitable** Ben Franklin was surely one of a kind.

15. The ability to reason is an **innate** characteristic of Homo sapiens.

16. Teenagers seem to have **insatiable** appetites.

17. I've always found her **inscrutable** because she never shows her feelings.

18. Although he made every effort to be charming, I could tell that his compliments were **insincere**.

19. She asked her husband to take her home early, for she had an **insufferable** headache.

20. He prefers to be **interred**, while she prefers cremation.

Fine words! I wonder where you stole 'em.
—Jonathan Swift

WORD	DEFINITION	ASSOCIATION *Create and write your associations in the spaces provided!*
1. **incipient** (in-sip-ient) adj.	beginning; commencing	______
2. **inclusive** (in-kloo-siv) adj.	including what is mentioned	______
3. **incorrigible** (in-kor-i-ji-bel) adj.	incapable of being corrected or reformed; hopeless	______
4. **indigenous** (in-dig-e-nus) adj.	native; originating in a particular place or country	______
5. **indolent** (in-do-lent) adj.	lazy; idle; avoiding exertion	______
6. **indubitably** (in-doo-bi-ta-blee) adj.	unquestionably; without reasonable doubt	______
7. **inept** (in-ept) adj.	not apt or fit; bungling	______
8. **infernal** (in-fur-nal) adj.	pertaining to hell; fiendish	______
9. **influx** (in-fluks) n.	act of flowing in	______
10. **infringe** (in-frinj) v.	encroach upon; violate; transgress	______
11. **ingenious** (in-jeen-yus) adj.	marked by inventive genius; cleverly contrived	Picture: the **mark** of a **genius** will be his **clever ideas**.
12. **ingenuous** (in-jen-yoo-us) adj.	naive; unsophisticated	______
13. **ingest** (in-jest) v.	take in; absorb; eat	______
14. **inimitable** (in-nim-i-ta-bel) adj.	surpassing imitation	______
15. **innate** (i-nayt) adj.	natural; native	______
16. **insatiable** (in-say-sha-bel) adj.	incapable of being satisfied; voracious	______
17. **inscrutable** (in-skroo-ta-bel) adj.	mysterious; incapable of being understood; baffling	______
18. **insincere** (in-sin-seer) adj.	false; hypocritical	______
19. **insufferable** (in-suf-e-ra-bel) adj.	unbearable; intolerably conceited or arrogant	______
20. **inter** (in-tur) v.	place in a grave or tomb	______

pan—all

See the **pan** with **all** the dishwasher **All** in it.

WORD ROOT	MEANING	ASSOCIATION *Create and write your associations in the spaces provided!*
PAN	**all**	See the **pan** with **all** the dishwasher **All** in it.
panorama (pan-o-ram-a) n.	an unlimited view in all directions.	
pantheism (pan-thee-iz-em) n.	doctrine that "God is all and all is God".	
panoply (pan-o-plee) n.	a splendid array.	
pandemonium (pan-de-moh-ni-um) n.	a place of uproar and confusion.	
panacea (pan-a-see-a) n.	a remedy for all kinds of diseases or troubles.	
pantheon (pan-thee-on) n.	a temple dedicated to all the gods.	
OMNI	**all**	______________________
omnipotent (om-nip-o-tent) adj.	having unlimited power.	
omnipresent (om-ni-praz-ent) adj.	present everywhere at the same time.	
omnivorous (om-niv-o-rus) adj.	eating all sorts of foods.	
omniscient (om-nish-ent) adj.	having knowledge of all things.	
omnify (om-ni-fi) v.	to cause to become universal.	
omnibus (om-ni-bus) n.	bus that carries a number of passengers, usually a fixed route.	
UNI	**one**	______________________
unity (yoo-ni-tee) n.	state of being one or a unit.	
universal (yoo-ni-vur-sal) adj.	used or understood by everyone.	
unique (yoo-neek) adj.	being the only one of its kind.	
unison (yoo-ni-son) n.	in agreement.	
university (yoo-ni-vur-si-tee) n.	educational institution composed of one or more colleges.	
unanimity (yoo-na-nim-i-tee) n.	agreeing completely.	

REVIEW

Draw a line between the word and its correct definition.

1. **incipient**
2. **insufferable**
3. **innate**
4. **inimitable**
5. **indubitably**
6. **inclusive**
7. **insincere**
8. **inscrutable**
9. **ingest**
10. **ingenuous**
11. **inept**
12. **indolent**
13. **incorrigible**

a. to take in
b. incapable of being understood
c. without a doubt
d. bungling
e. commencing
f. unbearable
g. natural
h. lazy
i. including what is mentioned
j. hypocritical
k. incapable of being corrected
l. naive
m. something without an equal

Circle the correct word below each definition.

1. **unlimited view in all directions**
   (panoply, pantheon, panorama, pancreas)
2. **cleverly contrived**
   (ingenuous, insular, integral, ingenious)
3. **incapable of being satisfied**
   (infantile, incubation, insatiable, insalubrious)
4. **pertaining to hell**
   (infamous, infernal, inflammatory, inflective)
5. **to transgress**
   (inebriate, indemnify, infringe, innervate)
6. **complete agreement**
   (animosity, unanimity, umlaut, unwieldy)
7. **to place in a grave**
   (intern, inhibit, inter, infuriate)
8. **having knowledge of all things**
   (omnipotent, onomatopoeia, omniscient, omnivorous)
9. **pouring in**
   (incumbent, influx, infinitive, inherent)
10. **originating in a particular place**
    (inhabitable, indigenous, inscrutable, interloper)

29

interlope (in-ter-loep)—meddle, intrude or encroach upon the affairs of others
See her mom **intruding** while they are **in** trying **to elope**.

EXAMPLE OF USE

1. She wishes that her friends would not **interlope** into her private affairs.
2. They settled their lawsuit through an **intermediary**.
3. The two freeways **intersect** at the downtown interchange.
4. A child who tries to **intimidate** another is called a bully.
5. The **irrevocable** words spoken during an argument may be cause for regret later on.
6. The strip of land that forms the **Isthmus** of Panama is the site of the Panama Canal.
7. Most of the produce is harvested by **itinerant** farm workers.
8. She asked her boss to give her an **itinerary** of his trip before leaving the office.
9. Children can sometimes be cruel by **jeering** at a clumsy classmate.
10. The politician's divorce **jeopardized** his career in politics.
11. His **judicial** appointment to the Superior Court was announced yesterday.
12. The two lawyers discussed the fine points of **jurisprudence**.
13. She bought a fourteen-**karat** gold bracelet for her bridesmaid.
14. He uprighted his **kayak** with ease when it turned over in the water.
15. Their common interests proved them to be **kindred** spirits.
16. The shoplifter turned out to be a **kleptomaniac**.
17. The view from the grassy **knoll** was breathtaking.
18. He earned the **kudos** bestowed upon him by the movie industry.
19. A little knowledge in the hands of the **laity** can be a dangerous thing.
20. The dissenters **lambasted** the politician with harsh words.

Don't grunt said Alice: That's not a proper way of expressing yourself.
—Lewis Carroll, *Alice in Wonderland*, ch. 6

WORD	DEFINITION	ASSOCIATION *Create and write your associations in the spaces provided!*
1. **interlope** (in-ter-loip) v.	meddle; intrude or encroach upon the affairs of others	See her mom **intruding** while they are **in** trying **to elope**.
2. **intermediary** (in-ter-mee-di-er-ee) n.	go-between; agent	______
3. **intersect** (in-ter-sekt) v.	overlap; have one or more points in common	______
4. **intimidate** (in-tim-i-dayt) v.	frighten; subdue with threats of force	______
5. **irrevocable** (i-rev-o-ka-bel) adj.	not capable of being recalled; final	______
6. **isthmus** (is-mus) n.	narrow strip of land bordered by water	______
7. **itinerant** (i-tin-e-rant) adj.	traveling from place to place	______
8. **itinerary** (i-tin-e-rer-ee) n.	plan of travel; list of places during journey	______
9. **jeer** (jeer) v.	scoff; sneer; laugh at rudely	______
10. **jeopardize** (jep-ar-diz) v.	endanger; expose to peril	______
11. **judicial** (joo-dish-al) adj.	the administration of justice	______
12. **jurisprudence** (joor-is-proo-dens) n.	science or philosophy of law	______
13. **karat** (kar-at) n.	twenty-fourth part of pure gold, to measure purity	______
14. **kayak** (ki-ak) n.	lightweight canoe, for one canoer, originating in Alaska	______
15. **kindred** (kin-drid) n.	relatives; family; of similar kind	______
16. **kleptomaniac** (klep-to-may-ni-ak) n.	one who steals without economic need	______
17. **knoll** (nohl) n.	small, rounded hill; mound	______
18. **kudos** (koo-dohz) n.	glory; fame; renown	______
19. **laity** (lay-i-tee) n.	those outside of profession, as opposed to those within it	______
20. **lambaste** (lam-bayst) v.	beat severely; thrash; blast	______

clam, claim—cry out, call out, declare
See the **clam crying out** of its clam shell.

WORD ROOT	MEANING	ASSOCIATION *Create and write your associations in the spaces provided!*
CLAM, CLAIM	**cry out, call out, declare**	See the **clam crying out** its **clam** shell.
clamor (klam-or) n.	loud protest or demand.	
exclamation (ek-skla-may-shon) n.	word or words cried out suddenly.	
claimant (klay-mant) n.	person who makes a claim.	
proclamation (prok-la-may-shon) n.	public declaration.	
unclaimed (un-klaymd) adj.	not taken.	
acclaim (a-klaym) v.	to greet with shouts of approval, applause.	
ROGA, ROG	**ask, beg**	______________________
interrogate (in-ter-o-gayt) v.	to ask questions of.	
derogative (de-rog-a-tiv) adj.	disparaging, contemptuous.	
abrogate (ab-ro-gayt) v.	to cancel or repeal.	
prerogative (pri-rog-a-tiv) n.	right or privilege belonging to a particular person or group.	
surrogate (sur-o-git) n.	substitute; deputy.	
arrogant (ar-o-gant) adj.	proud and overbearing through an exaggerated feeling of one's superiority.	
VOC, VOK	**voice, call**	______________________
vocal (voh-kal) adj.	uttered by the voice.	
vociferous (voh-sif-e-rus) adj.	making a great outcry.	
evoke (i-vohk) v.	to call up or inspire.	
vocabulary (voh-kab-uy-ler-ee) n.	list of words with their meanings.	
convocation (kon-vo-kay-shon) n.	an assembly summoned.	
invocation (in-vo-kay-shon) n.	calling upon God in prayer.	

REVIEW

Mark true or false in the space provided.

1. ________ A **surrogate** is someone who takes the place of another.
2. ________ To **lambaste** is to pour gravy on the meat.
3. ________ An **invocation** is an assembly of people summoned for a purpose.
4. ________ A **proclamation** is a public declaration.
5. ________ To **jeer** at someone is to look at him with ill will.
6. ________ An **irrevocable** act is something that can't be undone.
7. ________ The **laity** is the complete outfit for a newborn baby.
8. ________ An **itinerary** is a list of places one will go on a journey.
9. ________ To **intimidate** is to hint or imply something personal.
10. ________ A **kleptomaniac** is someone who steals compulsively.

Mark the letter from column 2 that best describes each word in column 1.

1		2
interlope	________	a. overlap
jurisprudence	________	b. narrow strip of land bordered by water
intersect	________	c. pertaining to administration of justice
kudos	________	d. expose to peril
kindred	________	e. a unit of weight for precious stones
isthmus	________	f. a go-between
jeopardize	________	g. credit for an achievement
knoll	________	h. one who travels place to place
kayak	________	i. to meddle
judicial	________	j. the philosophy of law
itinerant	________	k. of similar kind
intermediary	________	l. small, rounded hill
karat	________	m. lightweight canoe

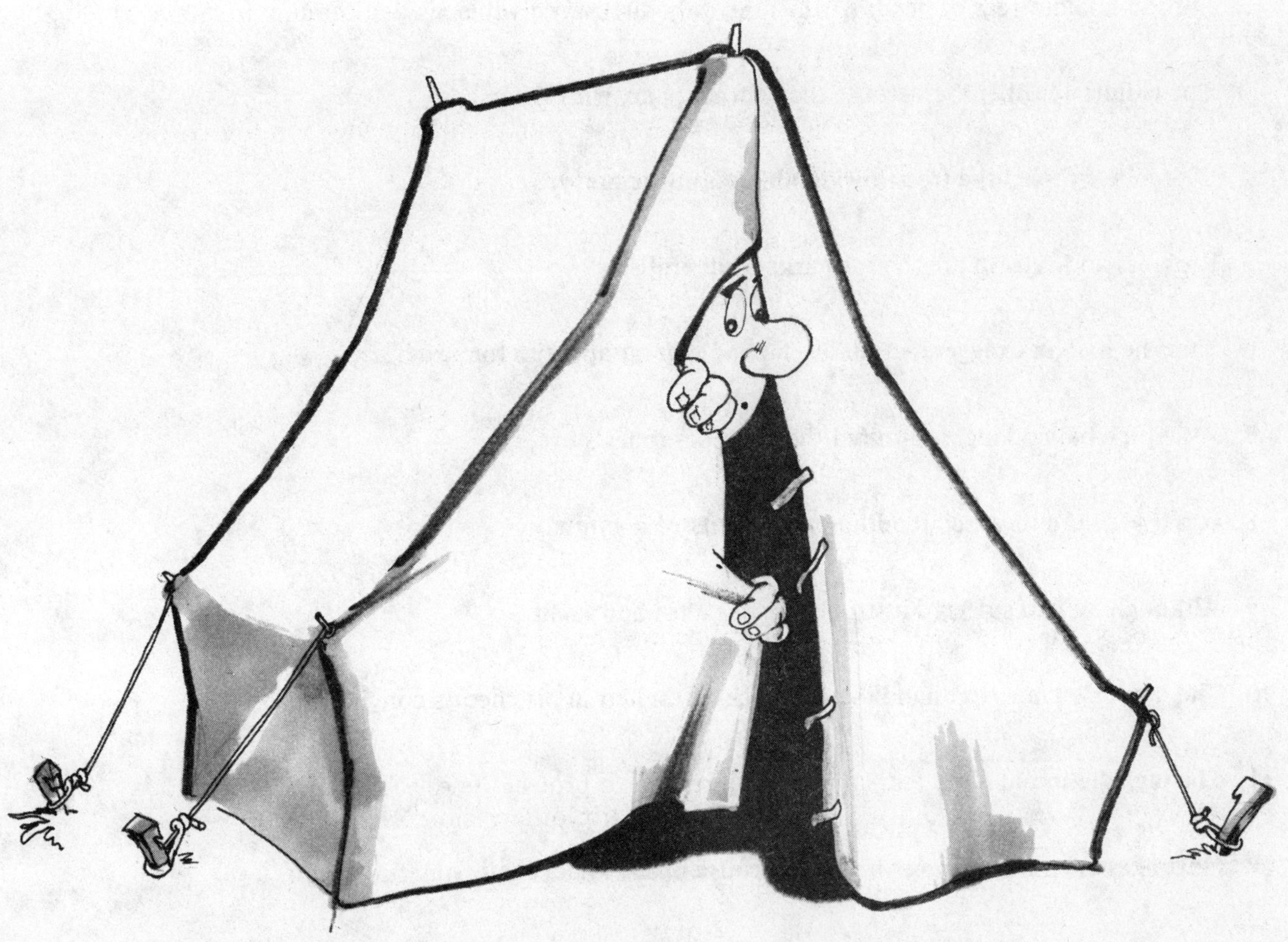

latent (lay-tent)—hidden, dormant
Imagine the **doorman hiding** in the **tent** when he was **late**.

EXAMPLE OF USE

1. The voluptuous woman constantly received **lascivious** looks.

2. He had a **latent** fear of heights, which he only discovered while visiting the Empire State Building.

3. The children misbehave because their father is **lax** with them.

4. Everyone enjoyed the free-flowing **libation** at the party.

5. Progress and reform are the earmarks of **liberalism**.

6. Since he had an exaggerated **libido**, he had a great appetite for sex.

7. A **lissome** ballet dancer captured the choreographer's eye.

8. It is a pleasure to watch the **lithe** movements of a gymnast.

9. Although he had suffered a stroke, he was alert and **lucid**.

10. The lawyer's **maladroit** handling of the case resulted in his client's conviction.

11. The **malediction** in King Tut's tomb was intended to protect the ruler's remains.

12. He makes enemies wherever he goes because of his **malevolent**, spiteful nature.

13. The locker room smelled of **malodorous** socks.

14. Through political **manipulation** he secured a position in the government.

15. The **martinet** trained his sons to behave like little soldiers.

16. Miss Lillian Carter is the **matriarch** of the Carter family.

17. The youth said it was his mother's nagging that prompted him to commit **matricide**.

18. A babbling brook **meanders** through the field behind the house.

19. It was his **megalomania** that drove Hitler to try to rule the world.

20. Los Angeles and New York are **megalopolises**.

With words we govern men.
—Disraeli

	WORD	DEFINITION	ASSOCIATION *Create and write your associations in the spaces provided!*
1.	**lascivious** (la-siv-i-us) adj.	lustful; lecherous; wanton	______
2.	**latent** (lay-tant) adj.	hidden, dormant	Imagine the **doorman hiding** in **tent** when he was **late**.
3.	**lax** (laks) adj.	slack; loose; not strict	______
4.	**libation** (li-bay-shon) n.	beverage; alcoholic drink	______
5.	**liberalism** (lib-e-ral-ezm) n.	political philosophy—with belief in change	______
6.	**libido** (li-bee-doh) n.	sexual drive	______
7.	**lissome** (lis-om) adj.	limber; flexible; agile	______
8.	**lithe** (lith) adj.	easily bent; supple; graceful	______
9.	**lucid** (loo-sid) adj.	clear; transparent; easy to understand	______
10.	**maladroit** (mal-a-droit) adj.	awkward; bungling	______
11.	**malediction** (mal-e-dik-shon) n.	evil statement or curse	______
12.	**malevolent** (ma-lev-o-lent) adj.	wishing harm to others; malicious	______
13.	**malodorous** (mal-oh-do-rus) adj.	offensive odor	______
14.	**manipulate** (ma-nip-yu-layt) v.	contrive to influence for advantage	______
15.	**martinet** (mahr-ti-net) n.	person who demands strict discipline.	______
16.	**matriarch** (may-tri-ahrk) n.	woman who is head of family or tribe	______
17.	**matricide** (mat-ri-sid) n.	act of killing one's mother	______
18.	**meander** (mee-an-der) v.	winding course; wander in a leisurely way	______
19.	**megalomania** (meg-a-loh-may-ni-a) n.	mania for exalted behavior	______
20.	**megalopolis** (meg-a-lop-o-lis) n.	very large city	______

jac, jec—throw
See **Jack throw** his **jacket**.

WORD ROOT	MEANING	ASSOCIATION *Create and write your associations in the spaces provided!*
JAC, JECT	**throw**	See **Jack throw** his **jacket**.
eject (i-jekt) v.	thrust or send out forcefully.	
inject (in-jekt) v.	to force or drive into something.	
conjecture (kon-jek-chor) v.	to guess.	
interjection (in-ter-jek-shon) n.	to throw in a remark when someone is speaking.	
adjective (aj-ik-tiv) n.	word added to a noun to describe the word.	
dejection (de-jek-shon) n.	a lowness of spirits.	
TRACT, TRAH	**draw, pull**	______________________________
attract (a-trakt) v.	to draw toward itself by unseen force.	
contract (kon-trakt) v.	to make smaller or shorter.	
protract (proh-trakt) v.	to prolong in duration, draw out.	
traction (trak-shon) n.	pulling or drawing a load along a surface.	
extract (ik-strakt) v.	to take out by force or effort.	
distract (di-strakt) v.	to draw away the attention of.	
PEND, PEN	**hand**	______________________________
independent (in-di-pen-dent) adj.	not controlled by another.	
impending (im-pend-ing) adj.	hanging or suspended.	
pendant (pen-dant) n.	hanging ornament.	
appendix (a-pen-diks) n.	section with supplementary information at the end of a book or document.	
suspension (su-spen-shon) n.	hanging.	
interdependent (in-ter-di-pen-dent) adj.	depends on each other.	

REVIEW

Mark the letter of the correct word for each definition in the space provided.

1. **to guess**
   a. contemporize b. conglomerate c. conjecture ________
2. **person who demands discipline**
   a. martinet b. marionette c. marsupial ________
3. **sexual drive**
   a. libation b. libido c. libertine ________
4. **hanging ornament**
   a. penchant b. periwinkle c. pendant ________
5. **awkward**
   a. malcontent b. maladroit c. malevolent ________
6. **act of killing one's mother**
   a. matriarchy b. matricide c. matrimony ________
7. **something that smells offensive**
   a. malicious b. malodorous c. malleable ________
8. **to draw attention away from**
   a. abstract b. protract c. distract ________
9. **a very large city**
   a. megalopolis b. megaton c. megaphone ________
10. **to be limber or agile**
   a. lipase b. lissome c. lithic ________

Mark the letter or write the word that best completes each sentence.

1. The defeat of numerous Democrats may spell the end of ____________.
   a. libretto b. libertinism c. liberalism
2. Students who do poorly on tests are often ____________ in their studies.
   a. libidinous b. lax c. leguminous
3. Anyone with delusions of grandeur suffers from ____________.
   a. menopause b. megalomania c. melancholia
4. W.C. Fields was famous for enjoying a ____________ now and then.
   a. leviathan b. libretto c. libation
5. Adolf Hitler is considered one of the most ____________ men of all times.
   a. magnanimous b. malevolent c. malleolus
6. Propaganda is a tool used to ____________ people.
   a. manifest b. manipulate c. malaise
7. People who don't know where they are going tend to ____________ through life.
   a. malleate b. maneuver c. meander
8. The quiet boy in the corner has ____________ tendencies toward violence.
   a. lateral b. latent c. languorous
9. Before the murderer was shot, he shouted a ____________ back at the police.
   a. malady b. malediction c. malaise
10. There are still some societies in which the ____________ controls the family.
   a. matrix b. maelstrom c. matriarch
11. It is considered ____________ for a man to chase after women all the time.
   a. lacerable b. lackadaisical c. lascivious
12. After suffering a stroke, the man's statements were no longer ____________.
   a. locative b. lucrative c. lucid
13. The young ballerina moved across the stage in a ____________ presentation of her skills.
   a. litmus b. liturgical c. lithe

31

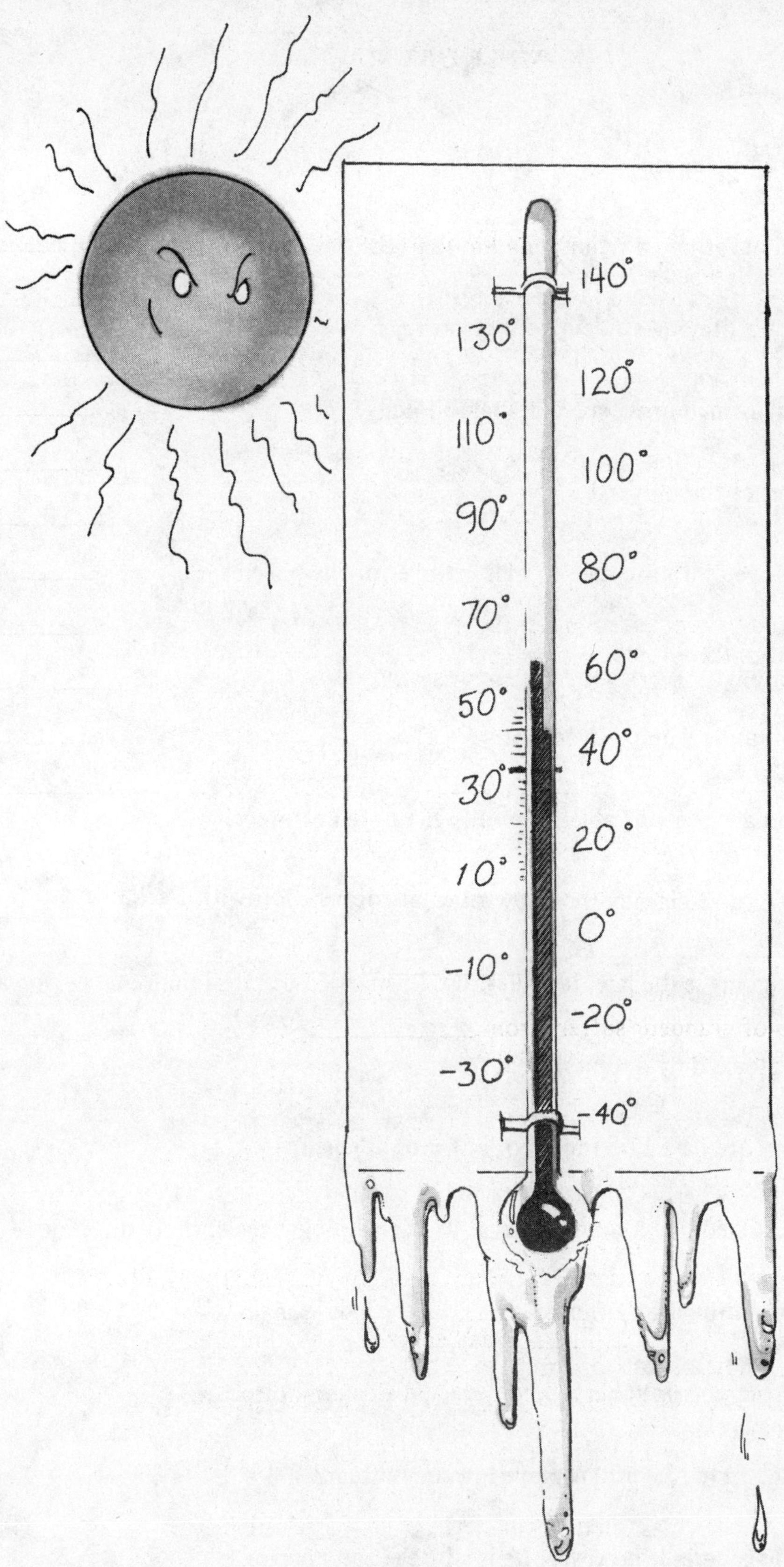

mercurial (mer-kyoor-i-all)—fickle, changing moods

Picture the **mercury** in the thermometer **changing moods**.

EXAMPLE OF USE

1. This family is a close-knit **menage**.
2. She's so **mercurial,** you never know from one minute to the next what her mood will be.
3. The local weatherman is a lifelong student of **meteorology**.
4. Scientific research is performed using specific **methodology**.
5. An atom is a **microcosm** of the universe.
6. The **migrant** workers moved into the area to pick lettuce for the market.
7. A hermit is usually a **misanthrope**.
8. The **misogynist** vowed that he would never marry.
9. Through tact and diplomacy she was able to **mollify** the irate customer.
10. England is an example of a **monarchy** that now rules in cooperation with Parliament.
11. In societies where **monogamy** is the law, it is illegal to be married to more than one person at the same time.
12. The cave entrance was blocked by a **monolith**.
13. Judaism and Christianity are based on the theory of **monotheism**.
14. Although the alien functioned like a human being, its **morphology** was entirely different.
15. An exaggerated sense of **nationalism** often leads a country into war.
16. A person who suffers from **necrophobia** would never be a funeral director.
17. Many tools from the **Neolithic** Age are displayed in the museum.
18. My grandfather is a **nonagenarian**; however, he is still alert and active.
19. He does not work as fast as more experienced men, for he is a **novice**.
20. Her belief in **numerology** caused her to stop dating the man.

Speak clearly, if you speak at all; Carve every word before you let it fall.
—Oliver Wendell Holmes, *A Rhymed Lesson*, 1. 408.

WORD	DEFINITION	ASSOCIATION *Create and write your associations in the spaces provided!*
1. **menage** (may-nahzh) n.	household or members of a household	______
2. **mercurial** (mer-kyoor-i-al) adj.	fickle, changing moods	Picture the **mercury** in the thermometer **changing moods**.
3. **meteorology** (mee-ti-o-rol-o-jee) n.	science dealing with motions of Earth's atmosphere	______
4. **methodology** (meth-o-dol-o-jee) n.	a particular procedure or set of procedures	______
5. **microcosm** (mi-kro-koz-em) n.	one unit that resembles a larger unit	______
6. **migrant** (mi-grant) n.	wanderer; migratory	______
7. **misanthrope** (mis-an-throp) n.	one who hates mankind	______
8. **misogynist** (mi-soj-i-nist) n.	one who hates women	______
9. **mollify** (mol-i-fi) v.	pacify; soothe; appease the anger of	______
10. **monarchy** (mon-ar-kee) n.	form of government—power is held by single ruler	______
11. **monogamy** (mo-nog-a-mee) n.	marriage to only one person at a time	______
12. **monolith** (mon-o-lith) n.	single large block or piece of stone, usually upright	______
13. **monotheism** (mon-o-thee-iz-em) n.	belief that there is only one God	______
14. **morphology** (mor-fol-o-jee) n.	study of structure and form of animals, plants	______
15. **nationalism** (nash-o-na-liz-em) n.	devotion to a nation; a movement favoring independence	______
16. **necrophobia** (nik-ro-foh-bi-a) n.	abnormal fear of death or dead bodies	______
17. **neolithic** (nee-o-lith-ik) adj.	belonging to an outmoded era; of later Stone Age	______
18. **nonagenarian** (non-a-je-nair-i-an) n.	one who is between 90 and 100 years of age	______
19. **novice** (nov-is) n.	inexperienced; beginner	______
20. **numerology** (noo-me-rol-o-jee) n.	study of the occult meaning of numbers	______

greg—flock, herd
In the **flock** or **herd**, all our names are **Greg**.

WORD ROOT	MEANING	ASSOCIATION *Create and write your associations in the spaces provided!*
GREG	**flock, herd**	In this **flock** or **herd**, all our names are **Greg**!
congregation (kong-gre-gay-shon) n.	group of people gathered together for religious worship.	
aggregate (ag-re-git) adj.	total, amount brought together.	
gregarious (gre-gar-i-us) adj.	living in flocks; fond of company.	
egregious (i-gree-jus) adj.	outstandingly bad.	
segregate (seg-re-gayt) v.	to put apart from the rest.	
desegregate (dee-seg-re-gayt) v.	to abolish racial segregation in public places.	
HABIT, HAB	**have, live**	______________________
inhabit (in-hab-it) v.	to live in a place as one's home.	
habitat (hab-i-tat) n.	natural environment of an animal or plant.	
habitual (ha-bich-oo-al) adj.	done regularly.	
rehabilitate (ree-ha-bil-i-tayt) v.	to restore a person to a normal life by training.	
haberdashery (hab-er-dash-e-ree) n.	store of small items of men's clothing.	
habeas corpus (hay-bi-as kor-pus)	Latin = you must have the body.	
VIV, VITA	**alive, life**	______________________
vital (vy-tal) adj.	necessary to life.	
vitamin (vy-ta-min) n.	organic substance essential to the nutrition of man and animals.	
revive (ri-vyv) v.	to bring back to life.	
survive (sir-vyv) v.	to continue to live or exist.	
vivacious (vy-vay-shus) adj.	lively, high-spirited.	
vivisect (viv-i-sekt) v.	performance of surgical experiment on living animals.	

REVIEW

Draw a line between the word and its correct definition.

1. **novice**	a. set of procedures
2. **nonagenarian**	b. one who hates women
3. **morphology**	c. inexperienced
4. **mollify**	d. belief in one God
5. **misanthrope**	e. study of the structure of animals and plants
6. **mercurial**	f. someone between 90 and 100 years of age
7. **methodology**	g. abnormal fear of death
8. **migrant**	h. changing moods
9. **misogynist**	i. one who hates mankind
10. **monotheism**	j. person who moves from place to place
11. **necrophobia**	k. to soothe
12. **monarchy**	l. government with one ruler
13. **neolithic**	m. belonging to the later Stone Age

Circle the correct word below each definition.

1. **a large, upright piece of stone**
   (monograph, monostrophe, monolith, monotype)
2. **to restore a person to a normal life**
   (habituate, rehabilitate, necromancy, metaphysics)
3. **members of a household**
   (mentor, mercenary, metier, menage)
4. **fond of company**
   (egregious, gregarious, neophyte, nocturnal)
5. **to perform surgical experiments on living animals**
   (nepenthe, nullify, vivisect, venerate)
6. **an event that represents something larger**
   (macrocosm, cosmology, microcosm, molecular)
7. **study of the occult meaning of numbers**
   (numismatics, numerology, nimbus, nunciature)
8. **marriage to one person at a time**
   (misogyny, monotheism, monogamy, morphology)
9. **devotion to one's country**
   (narcissism, narcolepsy, nationalism, nationalization)
10. **science dealing with the Earth's atmosphere**
    (meridean, metaphysics, metonymy, meteorology)

obstreperous (ob-strep-e-rus)—noisy, unruly

He got **strep** throat from being so **noisy** and **unruly**.

32

EXAMPLE OF USE

1. He tried to **obliterate** the memory, but no matter how hard he tried, he couldn't forget.
2. Her furious **obloquy** caused the child to shake all over.
3. Electric typewriters are making manual ones **obsolescent**.
4. His **obstreperous** behavior was partly due to the amount of alcohol he had consumed.
5. The wall will **occlude** the view of the ocean.
6. Marine biology is included in the study of **oceanography**.
7. The old-fashioned floor tiles were shaped like small **octagons**.
8. Although grandmother is an **octogenarian**, she is spry and full of life.
9. Bees are more attracted to **odoriferous** flowers than to those with no scent.
10. He hides behind sunglasses so that he can **ogle** the pretty girls in their bikinis.
11. The country was ruled by an **oligarchy** of wealthy landowners.
12. My father is the **omnipotent** head of our family.
13. Humans are **omnivorous** as a rule; they eat both animal and plant foods.
14. The **ophthalmologist** checked my eyes for possible cataracts.
15. The mouth is one of several bodily **orifices**.
16. Birdwatchers are lay experts in **ornithology**.
17. The **orthodontist** removed the braces from her teeth.
18. **Orthodox** methods of treatment have failed to cure his high blood pressure.
19. Her expertise in **orthography** makes her an excellent proofreader.
20. The child's slight birth defect was corrected easily through **orthopedics**.

WORD	DEFINITION	ASSOCIATION *Create and write your associations in the spaces provided!*
1. **obliterate** (o-blit-e-rayt) v.	destroy; remove all clear traces of	______
2. **obloquy** (ob-lo-kwee) n.	abusive, condemning speech	______
3. **obsolescent** (ob-so-les-ent) adj.	going out of use or fashion	______
4. **obstreperous** (ob-strep-e-rus) adj.	noisy, unruly	He got bad **strep** throat from being so **noisy** and **unruly**.
5. **occlude** (o-klood) v.	to shut in or out; obstruct	______
6. **oceanography** (oh-sha-nog-ra-fee) n.	physical geography dealing with the ocean	______
7. **octagon** (ok-ta-gon) n.	geometric figure with eight sides	______
8. **octogenarian** (ok-to-je-nair-i-an) n.	one who is between 80 and 90 years of age	______
9. **odoriferous** (oh-do-rif-a-rus) adj.	giving odor, usually a sweet scent; perfumed	______
10. **ogle** (oh-gel) v.	to look at amorously	______
11. **oligarchy** (ol-i-gahr-kee) n.	government ruled by exclusive class	______
12. **omnipotent** (om-nip-o-tent) adj.	possessing unlimited power, or very great power	______
13. **omnivorous** (om-niv-o-rus) adj.	eating both animal and plant foods	______
14. **ophthalmologist** (of-thal-mol-o-jist) n.	doctor of medicine—specializing in the eyes	______
15. **orifice** (or-i-fis) n.	mouthlike hole or vent	______
16. **ornithology** (or-ni-thol-o-jee) n.	branch of zoology relating to study of birds	______
17. **orthodontist** (or-tho-don-tist) n.	dentist specializing in the correction of teeth	______
18. **orthodox** (or-tho-doks) adj.	conventional; approved	______
19. **orthography** (or-thog-ra-fee) n.	correct spelling	______
20. **orthopedics** (or-tho-pee-diks) n.	branch of medicine dealing with skeletal deformities	______

pot, poss—power

See the **powerful** witch boil the **possum** in the **pot**.

WORD ROOT	MEANING	ASSOCIATION *Create and write your associations in the spaces provided!*
POT, POSS	**power**	See the **powerful** witch boil the **possum** in the **pot**.
potent (poh-tent) adj.	having great natural power.	
omnipotent (om-nip-o-tent) adj.	having unlimited power.	
potential (po-ten-shal) adj.	capable of being developed or used.	
potentate (poh-ten-tayt) n.	monarch or ruler.	
impotent (im-po-tent) adj.	powerless, unable to take action.	
posse (pos-ee) n.	a body of men legally empowered to assist a sheriff.	
DYN, DYNAMO	**power**	________________
dynamic (dy-nam-ik) adj.	force producing motion.	
dynamite (dy-na-myt) n.	powerful explosive made of nitro.	
dynasty (dy-na-stee) n.	line of hereditary rulers.	
dynamo (dy-na-moh) n.	compact generator producing electric current.	
dynamometer (dy-na-mom-e-ter) n.	an instrument for measuring force or energy.	
dyne (dine) n.	a unit of force.	
VALI, VALE	**strength, worth**	________________
valid (val-id) adj.	having legal force.	
valiant (val-yant) adj.	brave, courageous.	
evaluate (i-val-yoo-ayt) v.	to assess the value of.	
equivalent (i-kwiv-a-lent) adj.	equal in value or importance.	
valor (val-or) n.	bravery, especially in fighting.	
valetude (val-e-tood) n.	attention to preserving health.	

REVIEW

Mark true or false in the space provided.

1. ________ A **potentate** is an exceptionally strong remedy.
2. ________ **Ornithology** is the study of the eye and its care.
3. ________ A **dynasty** is a line of hereditary rulers.
4. ________ **Obloquy** is a verbal presentation of praise.
5. ________ A **valiant** officer exhibits courage in his actions.
6. ________ An **ophthalmologist** is concerned with skeletal deformities.
7. ________ An omnivorous **diet** consists of vegetables and meat.
8. ________ An **oligarchy** is a government in oil-rich countries.
9. ________ **Oceanography** is the geographical study of oceans.
10. ________ An **octagon** is a mollusk related to the octopus.

Mark the letter from column 2 that best describes each word in column 1.

1		2
obliterate	________	a. possessing unlimited power
orthopedics	________	b. to shut in or out
orifice	________	c. mouthlike vent
orthography	________	d. conventional
orthodox	________	e. to look at amorously
orthodontist	________	f. someone 80 to 90 years old
omnipotent	________	g. noisy
ogle	________	h. going out of use
occlude	________	i. correct spelling
octogenarian	________	j. to remove all traces of
obsolescent	________	k. giving out odor
obstreperous	________	l. study of skeletal deformities
odoriferous	________	m. dentist who corrects tooth development

33

penury (pen-yu-ree)—extreme poverty
See someone **so poor** that he only has one **penny** left.

EXAMPLE OF USE

1. The bouncer will **oust** the two men if they begin to fight.

2. His interest in **paleontology** began when he found a fossilized fish.

3. When she feels ill, her face develops a **pallid** look.

4. The **panorama** of the Rocky Mountains is breathtaking.

5. The **paradox** is that the whole town admires the scoundrel, even though he robbed them blind.

6. Although many people still believe she's guilty, Lizzie Borden was cleared of charges of **parricide**.

7. He suffered from malnutrition because he was too **parsimonious** to buy the proper food or the vitamins he needed.

8. The hula hoop, once a fad, is now **passé**.

9. She gave her father a playful rap on his balding **pate**.

10. Researchers are constantly searching for the **pathogens** of diseases.

11. **Pathology** is an important science used in diagnosing diseases.

12. My **patrimony** includes my grandfather's homestead and grandmother's jewelry.

13. A new **pedagogue** was hired when the school enrollment went up.

14. He has a **pedant's** love of historical detail.

15. The **pellucid** lampshade cast bright, glowing light on the page.

16. When he paid off all his debts, he discovered he was going to be living in **penury**.

17. The couple love to **perambulate** through the park every day to feed the pigeons.

18. A picket fence marked the **perimeter** of the front yard.

19. Abe Lincoln **personified** honesty.

20. She works at every charity bazaar and is widely known for her **philanthropy**.

You may regret your silence once, but you will regret your words often.
—adapted from Ibn Gabirol

WORD	DEFINITION	ASSOCIATION *Create and write your associations in the spaces provided!*
1. **oust** (owst) v.	to turn out from a place or position occupied	
2. **paleontology** (pay-li-on-tol-o-jee) n.	science dealing with study of fossil remains	
3. **pallid** (pal-id) adj.	pale; wan; lacking sparkle or vitality	
4. **panorama** (pan-o-ram-a) n.	complete view over a wide area	
5. **paradox** (par-a-doks) n.	statement that seems to contradict itself	
6. **parricide** (par-i-sid) n.	one who murders a parent or other close relative	
7. **parsimonious** (pahr-si-moh-ni-as) adj.	excessively frugal; stingy	
8. **passé** (pa-say) adj.	outmoded; antiquated	
9. **pate** (payt) n.	the head	
10. **pathogen** (path-o-jen) n.	an agent (such as bacterium or virus) causing disease	
11. **pathology** (pa-thol-o-jee) n.	scientific study of diseases of the body	
12. **patrimony** (pat-ri-moh-nee) n.	anything inherited from one's ancestors, or heritage	
13. **pedagogue** (ped-a-gog) n.	school teacher	
14. **pedant** (ped-ant) n.	one who demands strict observance of formal rules	
15. **pellucid** (pe-loo-sid) adj.	capable of transmitting light; very clear	
16. **penury** (pen-yu-ree) adj.	extreme poverty	See someone **so poor** that he only has one **penny** left.
17. **perambulate** (per-am-byu-layt) v.	to walk through, about or over	
18. **perimeter** (pe-rim-e-ter) n.	outer boundary of a two-dimensional figure	
19. **personify** (per-son-i-fi) v.	to treat as a person; typify	
20. **philanthropy** (fi-lan-thro-pee) n.	goodwill toward humanity; love of mankind	

ten, tent—hold

See him **hold tent** number **ten**.

WORD ROOT	MEANING	ASSOCIATION *Create and write your associations in the spaces provided!*
TEN, TENT	**hold**	See him **hold tent** number **ten**.
intention (in-ten-shon) n.	what one plans to do or achieve.	
contented (kon-ten-tid) adj.	happy with what one has.	
tenacious (te-nay-shus) adj.	holding firmly to something.	
tenable (ten-a-bel) adj.	able to be held against attack.	
retentive (ri-ten-tiv) adj.	able to retain or hold things or ideas.	
maintenance (mayn-te-nans) n.	keep in good repair or existence.	
POS, POUND	**place, set**	______________________
positive (poz-i-tiv) adj.	leaving no room for doubt.	
posit (poz-it) v.	to present or assume as fact.	
composition (kom-po-zish-on) n.	putting together into a whole.	
expose (ik-spohz) v.	to leave a person or thing unprotected.	
expound (ik-spownd) v.	to set forth or explain in detail.	
impose (im-pohz) v.	to place a tax or obligation on.	
VER, VERI	**true, genuine**	______________________
verify (ver-i-fy) v.	check the truth or correctness of.	
verity (ver-i-tee) n.	the truth of something.	
veracious (ve-ray-shus) adj.	truthful, true.	
veritable (ver-i-ta-bel) adj.	real, rightly named.	
verisimilitude (ver-i-si-mil-i-tood) n.	an appearance of being true.	
verdict (ver-dikt) n.	decision reached by a jury.	

REVIEW

Mark the letter of the correct word for each definition in the space provided.

1. **excessively frugal**
   a. pathological b. parsimonious c. perspicacious ________
2. **an appearance of being true**
   a. variegated b. vernacular c. verisimilitude ________
3. **the study of fossil remains**
   a. paleontology b. paraphernalia c. plagiarism ________
4. **a bacterial agent causing disease**
   a. peripatetic b. pathogen c. patina ________
5. **school teacher**
   a. pederast b. pedagogue c. perigrine ________
6. **extreme poverty**
   a. prehensile b. penury c. perdition ________
7. **the head**
   a. phalanx b. pate c. phlebotomy ________
8. **lacking sparkle or vitality**
   a. pandemic b. paltry c. pallid ________
9. **to represent something inanimate as a person**
   a. impersonate b. personify c. perspicacity ________
10. **to walk through**
    a. percolate b. perforate c. perambulate ________

Mark the letter or write the word that best completes each sentence.

1. The skyscraper yielded a wide __________ of the city.
   a. paraplegia b. parameter c. panorama
2. The rebels moved to __________ the incumbent president.
   a. ordain b. ovulate c. oust
3. The unpopular principal was regarded as a __________ by the teachers.
   a. palindrome b. pedant c. parabola
4. Among the stars, super novas are considered the most __________.
   a. pecuniary b. pellucid c. phlegmatic
5. The Nobel Prize is awarded on the basis of __________.
   a. phenomenology b. plebiscite c. philanthropy
6. The soldiers marched around the __________ of the fort.
   a. prosthesis b. perimeter c. preamble
7. These days, counter-culture lifestyles are considered __________.
   a. pavid b. pastern c. passé
8. All of the routine tests were completed in the __________ lab.
   a. patronymic b. pathology c. pituitary
9. The best kind of mind for vocabulary improvement is a __________ mind.
   a. reclusive b. redolent c. retentive
10. Very few individuals exist who would __________ that the Earth is flat.
    a. procreate b. posit c. impose
11. The distribution of the dead man's estate was a matter of __________.
    a. patroness b. pathogenesis c. patrimony
12. To kill a member of one's own family is an act of __________.
    a. panoply b. parricide c. pedicure
13. Most books in existential literature are dominated by the __________.
    a. panacea b. polymer c. paradox

34

pinnacle (pin-a-kel)—very topmost point, as of a mountain
See **pen-nickle peak** at the **topmost point** of the mountain.

EXAMPLE OF USE

1. Hot, humid weather can make the most energetic person become **phlegmatic**.

2. A **phobia** of the number 13 is based on superstition.

3. After the criminal was disarmed, his arms were **pinioned** behind his back.

4. The Nobel Prize is the **pinnacle** of achievement.

5. The **piquant** aromas issuing from the Italian restaurant had drawn many a diner in to sample the food.

6. The doting mother attempted to **placate** her angry child.

7. There was not a dry eye in the theatre after she sang the **plaintive** melody.

8. Clay is fun to work with because it is a **pliant** material.

9. She was charged with **polyandry** because she had failed to divorce each of her three prior husbands.

10. At one time the Mormon Church encouraged its members to practice **polygamy**.

11. He obtained the position of interpreter at the United Nations because he is a **polyglot**.

12. The religion of the ancient Greeks is a good example of **polytheism**.

13. The coroner's **post-mortem** examination determined that the girl died of natural causes.

14. Since the birth was a difficult one, the mother required extensive **postnatal** care.

15. As an afterthought, she added a **postscript** (P.S.) to the end of the letter to say she was enclosing pictures.

16. A **premonition** of danger caused him to avoid driving his car yesterday.

17. A deposit of $1,500 was a **prerequisite** to the sale of the house.

18. I don't believe a word she says because she has a reputation for **prevarication**.

19. Accuracy has its place, but he is so smug and narrow-minded as to be a **prig**.

20. **Promptitude** is no virtue on social occasions, as it is proper to arrive a little late.

Clear conception leads naturally to clear and correct expression.
—Boileau

WORD	DEFINITION	ASSOCIATION *Create and write your associations in the spaces provided!*
1. **phlegmatic** (fleg-mat-ik) adj.	impassive; stolid; stodgy	______________
2. **phobia** (foh-bi-a) n.	extreme, often inexplicable, fear	______________
3. **pinion** (pin-yon) v.	bind arms to the body to render helpless; shackle	______________
4. **pinnacle** (pin-a-kel) n.	very topmost point, as of a mountain	See **pen-nickle peak** at the **topmost point** of the mountain.
5. **piquant** (pee-kant) adj.	pleasantly sharp taste; keen interest	______________
6. **placate** (play-kayt) v.	appease; pacify; conciliate	______________
7. **plaintive** (playn-tiv) adj.	sad; melancholy	______________
8. **pliant** (ply-ant) adj.	flexible; supple; pliable	______________
9. **polyandry** (pol-i-an-dree) n.	system of having more than one husband at a time	______________
10. **polygamy** (po-lig-a-mee) n.	marriage with more than one wife concurrently	______________
11. **polyglot** (pol-i-glot) n.	one who understands many languages	______________
12. **polytheism** (pol-i-thee-iz-em) n.	belief in more than one god	______________
13. **post mortem** (pohst-mor-tem) adj.	after death, fact or event	______________
14. **postnatal** (pohst-nay-tal) adj.	after giving birth	______________
15. **postscript** (pohst-skript) n.	addition to written composition as an afterthought	______________
16. **premonition** (pree-mo-nish-on) n.	forewarning; omen	______________
17. **prerequisite** (pri-rek-wi-zit) adj.	condition required beforehand	______________
18. **prevaricate** (pri-var-i-kayt) v.	lie; act or speak evasively	______________
19. **prig** (prig) n.	self-righteous; overly precise	______________
20. **promptitude** (prompt-i-tood) adj.	promptness; alacrity; readiness	______________

luc, lum, lun—light

The **loose** (luc) **light lumped** (lum) him when it **landed** (lun).

WORD ROOT	MEANING	ASSOCIATION *Create and write your associations in the spaces provided!*
LUC, LUM, LUN	**light**	The **loose** (luc) **light lumped** (lum) him when it **landed** (lun).
lucid (loo-sid) adj.	expressed; easy to understand.	
pellucid (pe-loo-sid) adj.	very clear.	
elucidate (i-loo-si-dayt) v.	to throw light on; make clear.	
translucent (trans-loo-sent) adj.	allowing light to pass through, but not transparent.	
illuminate (i-loo-mi-nayt) v.	to light up, to make bright.	
luminescence (loo-mi-nes-ens) n.	light emitted without being hot.	
CALOR	**heat**	____________________
calorie (kal-o-ree) n.	unit for measuring quantity of heat.	
scald (skawld) v.	heat near boiling point.	
caloric (ka-lor-ik) adj.	of heat.	
calorimetry (kal-o-rim-e-tree) n.	method of measuring heat.	
calorescence (kal-o-res-ens) n.	the change of infrared radiant energy into visible light.	
calorific (kal-o-rif-ik) adj.	producing heat.	
HYDR, HYDRO, HYDRA	**water**	____________________
hydrant (hi-drant) n.	pipe from water main to attachment for fire hoses.	
dehydrate (dee-hi-drayt) v.	remove moisture from.	
hydrotherapy (hi-dro-ther-a-pee) n.	use of water in the treatment of disease.	
hydrostatic (hi-dro-stat-ik) adj.	pressure of water or other liquid at rest.	
hydraulic (hi-draw-lik) adj.	operating for movement of water.	
hydrophone (hi-dra-fon) n.	instrument for detecting and registering sound transmitted through water.	

REVIEW

Draw a line between the word and its correct definition.

1. **phlegmatic**	a. to pacify
2. **promptitude**	b. flexible
3. **postnatal**	c. after death
4. **phobia**	d. sad
5. **pliant**	e. belief in more than one god
6. **premonition**	f. self-righteous person
7. **plaintive**	g. keen interest
8. **piquant**	h. readiness
9. **prig**	i. extreme fear
10. **postscript**	j. addition to writing project
11. **post mortem**	k. forewarning
12. **polytheism**	l. accepting everything calmly
13. **placate**	m. after birth

Circle the correct word below each definition.

1. **to act or speak with concealment**
   (palpitate, precipitate, prevaricate, prognosticate)
2. **to make information clear**
   (elocute, elucidate, elegize, elate)
3. **the highest point**
   (nadir, picaresque, pinnacle, piquancy)
4. **producing heat**
   (caledonian, calorific, calliopean, calumnious)
5. **marriage with more than one wife concurrently**
   (polyandry, polyphagus, polytomy, polygamy)
6. **to remove moisture**
   (hydrolyze, delineate, dehydrate, deify)
7. **to bind up and render helpless**
   (placate, pilfer, pinion, precipitate)
8. **having more than one husband at a time**
   (polygamy, polonaise, polyandry, polyglot)
9. **condition required beforehand**
   (prefecture, premonition, prerequisite, preservative)
10. **one who understands many languages**
    (protagonist, polyglot, protégé, psychic)

35

quay (kay)—dock
See the sign that says "this **(q)way** to the **dock.**"

EXAMPLE OF USE

1. Five times a day, devout muslims **prostrate** themselves in prayer.

2. Samuel Clemens wrote many books under the **pseudonym** Mark Twain.

3. Sigmund Freud's work is famous in the field of **psychology**.

4. A **psychopath** is one of the most dangerous patients in a mental hospital.

5. Because of his **punctilious** manner, the butler has been employed by the upper echelons of society.

6. I could never be a war hero, for I am **pusillanimous**.

7. In ancient Greece funeral **pyres** were built to cremate the dead.

8. **Pyromania,** rather than accident, is responsible for much loss of property each year.

9. A person with **pyrophobia** would be reluctant to light a match.

10. Dogs, cats and horses are three examples of **quadrupeds**.

11. Amid the merriment, several men **quaffed** beer.

12. Using big words can make one a **quasi** scholar, but only through understanding those words can one become a true scholar.

13. We waited on the **quay** while they went out fishing.

14. Helen of Troy is said to have been the **quintessence** of beauty.

15. The **quondam** caterpillar is now a butterfly.

16. The city council **quorum** was present, so the voting took place.

17. Will Rogers was one of America's foremost **raconteurs**.

18. The costume director deserves credit for the magnificent **raiment** worn by King Lear.

19. The leader of the subversive group incited the members to go on a **rampage**.

20. The lard turned **rancid** and had to be thrown away.

Syllables govern the world.
—John Seldon, *Power*

WORD	DEFINITION	ASSOCIATION *Create and write your associations in the spaces provided!*
1. **prostrate** (pros-trayt) adj.	throw down; flatten; submit in reverence	______
2. **pseudonym** (soo-do-nim) n.	assumed name	______
3. **psychology** (si-kol-o-jee) n.	science of emotions, behavior and mind	______
4. **psychopath** (si-ko-path) n.	one who is severely disordered mentally	______
5. **punctilious** (pungk-til-i-us) adj.	excessively exact in the observance of rules	______
6. **pusillanimous** (pyoo-si-lan-i-mus) adj.	cowardly; timorous	______
7. **pyre** (pir) n.	pile of wood for burning corpses	______
8. **pyromania** (pi-ro-may-nia) n.	mania for setting things on fire	______
9. **pyrophobia** (pi-ro-fo-bee-ah) n.	morbid fear of fire	______
10. **quadruped** (kwod-ru-ped) n.	animal having four feet	______
11. **quaff** (kwahf) v.	drink greedily in long drafts	______
12. **quasi** (kway-zi) adj.	seemingly; apparently	______
13. **quay** (kay) n.	dock	See the sign that says "this **(q)way** to the **dock**."
14. **quintessence** (kwin-tes-ans) n.	pure and concentrated essence of a substance	______
15. **quondam** (kwon-dum) adj.	formerly; sometime	______
16. **quorum** (kwor-um) n.	number of members required to be present at a meeting	______
17. **raconteur** (rak-on-tur) n.	storyteller	______
18. **raiment** (ray-ment) n.	poetic term for clothing; garments	______
19. **rampage** (ram-payj) n.	excited action; violent behavior	______
20. **rancid** (ran-sid) adj.	rankly offensive to the senses; disgusting	______

hypo—under, sub, less

See the **hypo submerge under less** water than usual.

WORD ROOT	MEANING	ASSOCIATION *Create and write your associations in the spaces provided!*
HYPO	**under, sub, less**	See the **hypo submerge under less** water than usual.
hypothesis (hy-poth-e-sis) n.	a supposition put forward to be proved or unproved.	
hypodermic (hy-po-dur-mik) adj.	injected beneath the skin.	
hypochondriac (hy-po-kon-dri-ac) n.	person who is overly anxious about health.	
hypothetical (hy-po-thet-i-kal) adj.	supposed, but not necessarily true.	
hypoglycemia (hy-po-gly-see-mi-a) n.	abnormally low blood sugar.	
hypotension (hy-po-ten-shon) n.	abnormally low blood pressure.	
HYPER	**above, over, excessive**	______________________
hypersensitive (hy-per-sen-si-tiv) adj.	excessively sensitive.	
hypercritical (hy-per-krit-i-kal) adj.	excessively critical.	
hyperbole (hy-pur-bo-lee) n.	exaggerated statement not meant to be taken literally.	
hypersonic (hy-per-son-ik) adj.	speeds exceeding five times that of sound.	
hyperthermia (hy-per-ther-mi-a) n.	body temperature greatly above normal.	
hypertrophy (hy-pur-tro-fee) n.	organ enlargement caused by excessive nutrition.	
DIA	**through**	______________________
dialogue (dy-a-lawg) n.	conversation or discussion.	
diatribe (dy-a-tryb) n.	abusive criticism.	
diameter (dy-am-e-ter) n.	straight line passing through a circle from side to side.	
dialectic (dy-a-lek-tik) n.	investigation of philosophical truths.	
diathermy (dy-a-thur-mee) n.	heat treatment by passing electric current through the body.	
dialysis (dy-al-i-sis) n.	blood purification by flowing through a suitable membrane.	

REVIEW

Mark true or false in the space provided.

1. ________ To be **punctilious** is to be excessively precise.
2. ________ **Quintessence** is the study of quintuplets.
3. ________ A **quadruped** is a person whose arms and legs are paralyzed.
4. ________ **Hyperbole** is an exaggeration of the truth.
5. ________ Food left out too long begins to smell **rancid**.
6. ________ A **psychopath** is someone who can predict the future.
7. ________ **Dialysis** is a system of blood purification.
8. ________ **Raiment** is shell-fire over a battleground.
9. ________ **Hypoglycemia** is high blood sugar in the body.
10. ________ To be **pusillanimous** is to be especially aggressive.

Mark the letter from column 2 that best describes each word in column 1.

1		2
rampage	________	a. stretched out in submission
quorum	________	b. fear of fire
quasi	________	c. dock
prostrate	________	d. storyteller
pyre	________	e. formerly
quaff	________	f. violent behavior
raconteur	________	g. to drink greedily
quondam	________	h. number of members required at a meeting
pyromania	________	i. assumed name
quay	________	j. science of the mind
psychology	________	k. excitement for setting fires
pyrophobia	________	l. seemingly
pseudonym	________	m. pile of wood for burning corpses

reproof (re-proof)—blame
See the prosecutor say there is **proof** that he's to **blame**.

36

EXAMPLE OF USE

1. The **rapacious** victors seized more than just the spoils of war.

2. I couldn't sleep because of the **raucous** party next door.

3. The man declared his love but was met with a **rebuff.**

4. The speech ended with a **recapitulation** of the main points.

5. A water shortage was averted by the use of a **reclamation** plant.

6. Smart investment enabled him to **recoup** his losses and avoid bankruptcy.

7. The quarrel ended when she agreed to **rectify** the error she had made.

8. They bought an old house because they knew they would enjoy **refurbishing** it.

9. Warm saltwater is sometimes used to cause a patient to **regurgitate** harmful substances.

10. I was **remiss** in my social obligations by neglecting to send a "Thank You" card.

11. The judge ordered the defendant to make full **reparation** for the property he had destroyed.

12. "Sleeping Beauty lies there in sweet **repose.**"

13. A **reproach** is sometimes necessary to correct a child's behavior.

14. Let's not waste time on **reproofs,** but try to discover why the problem arose in the first place.

15. He **repudiates** what he doesn't understand.

16. Although they were outnumbered, the defenders of the castle **repulsed** the invaders.

17. The course is **requisite** to completing a college degree.

18. Robert Merrill of the Metropolitan Opera has a **resonant** voice.

19. In **retrospect,** I should have studied more before taking the exam.

20. Some older people **revert** to childlike behavior.

WORD	DEFINITION	ASSOCIATION *Create and write your associations in the spaces provided!*
1. **rapacious** (ra-pay-shus) adj.	extremely greedy; seizes to satisfy greed	________
2. **raucous** (raw-kuss) adj.	loud and harsh sound	________
3. **rebuff** (re-buf) n.	snub; put off with abrupt denial	________
4. **recapitulate** (ree-ka-pich-u-layt) v.	summary of principal facts	________
5. **reclamation** (rek-la-may-shun) n.	reclaiming for use or service	________
6. **recoup** (re-koop) v.	return; reimburse; recover	________
7. **rectify** (rek-ti-fi) v.	make right, remedy	________
8. **refurbish** (ree-fur-bish) v.	renovate; polish up	________
9. **regurgitate** (ri-gur-ji-tayt) v.	surge back; repeat exactly	________
10. **remiss** (re-mis) adj.	negligent; inattentive	________
11. **reparation** (rep-a-ray-shun) n.	repair a wrong; make amends; restitution	________
12. **repose** (ri-pohz) n.	rest; quiet; tranquility; sleep	________
13. **reproach** (ri-prohch) v.	severe expression of disapproval for a fault	________
14. **reproof** (re-proof) n.	blame	See the prosecutor say there is **proof** that he's to **blame**.
15. **repudiate** (ri-pyoo-di-ayt) v.	reject; refuse to acknowledge	________
16. **repulse** (ri-puls) v.	drive back; repel; reject	________
17. **requisite** (rek-wi-zit) adj.	that which is necessary	________
18. **resonant** (rez-o-nant) adj.	resounding; rich in sound	________
19. **retrospect** (ret-ro-spekt) n.	review of past events or time	________
20. **revert** (ri-vurt) v.	turn back; return to former habit or custom	________

miso—hate, bad, wrong

Miserable people are **bad** and **wrong** to **hate**!

WORD ROOT	MEANING	ASSOCIATION *Create and write your associations in the spaces provided!*
MISO	**hate, bad, wrong**	**Miserable** people are **bad** and **wrong** to **hate**!
misanthrope (mis-an-throhp) n.	one who dislikes people in general.	
misogynist (mi-soj-i-nist) n.	a person who hates women.	
misbehave (mis-bi-hayv) v.	to behave badly.	
misconception (mis-kon-sep-shon) n.	a wrong interpretation.	
miscreant (mis-kree-ant) n.	a wrongdoer, a villain.	
misadventure (mis-ad-ven-chur) n.	a piece of bad luck.	
VICT, VINC	**conquer**	____________________
victim (vik-tim) n.	a person injured or killed by another or as a result of an occurrence.	
victory (vik-to-ree) n.	success in battle or contest achieved by conquering one's opponents.	
convict (kon-vikt) v.	to prove a person guilty of a crime.	
invincible (in-vin-si-bel) adj.	unconquerable.	
evict (i-vikt) v.	to expel by legal process.	
vanquish (vang-kwish) v.	to conquer.	
PHIL, PHILO	**love**	____________________
philosophy (fi-los-o-fee) n.	system of principles for the conduct of life.	
philanthropist (fi-lan-thro-pist) n.	one who loves mankind.	
philogynist (fi-loj-o-nist) n.	person who loves women.	
philharmonic (fil-hahr-mon-ik) adj.	devoted to music.	
philatelist (fi-lat-e-list) n.	person who collects stamps.	
philanderer (fi-lan-der-er) n.	one who engages in a love affair without serious intent.	

REVIEW

Mark the letter of the correct word for each definition in the space provided.

1. **an evil person**
   a. mignon b. miscreant c. maverick ________
2. **review of past events**
   a. recession b. rapture c. retrospect ________
3. **person who collects stamps**
   a. philanderer b. philanthropist c. philatelist ________
4. **to surge back or repeat exactly**
   a. recriminate b. regurgitate c. repudiate ________
5. **one who cannot be conquered**
   a. invidious b. insidious c. invincible ________
6. **extremely greedy nature**
   a. rapturous b. rapacious c. reconnoiter ________
7. **a process of restoring use to certain elements**
   a. reclamation b. introspection c. recrimination ________
8. **to summarize principal facts on a subject**
   a. regurgitate b. recapitulate c. reinstate ________
9. **an abrupt denial of assistance**
   a. rebate b. rebuke c. rebuff ________
10. **a state of sleep or tranquility**
    a. recessional b. repose c. reprimand ________

Mark the letter or write the word that best completes each sentence.

1. His supporters were afraid that he might ___________ back to his old ways.
   a. reciprocate b. revert c. relegate
2. During the first world war, Germany was forced to make ___________ to the Allies.
   a. recognition b. reparation c. rampart
3. The audiophile down the street has a set of speakers with ___________ sound quality.
   a. redemptive b. remunerative c. resonant
4. The woman who was fired had been ___________ in her duties.
   a. risible b. remiss c. rational
5. It is possible to ___________ an old house to look like new.
   a. refurbish b. recalcitrate c. regiment
6. After the stock market collapsed, the man tried to ___________ his losses.
   a. renown b. recoup c. repertoire
7. The fraternity house was always the scene of ___________ laughter.
   a. residual b. reverential c. raucous
8. One ___________ to college admission is an extensive vocabulary.
   a. revery b. requisite c. recluse
9. The woman dressed in mannish attire to ___________ any sexual advances.
   a. remiss b. rehabilitate c. repulse
10. When the customer criticizes the product, a good manager attempts to ___________ the situation.
    a. regiment b. rectify c. reminisce
11. For those who commit a crime, a ___________ of wrongdoing is due.
    a. reprisal b. reproof c. requisition
12. Parents usually ___________ their children for mischievous behavior.
    a. rescind b. replenish c. reproach
13. Many citizens ___________ the Internal Revenue Service by refusing to submit an income tax return.
    a. regurgitate b. repudiate c. resuscitate

saturnine (sat-ur-nin)—gloomy, very serious appearance
See **Saturn** is a very **gloomy** planet.

EXAMPLE OF USE

1. You must first grasp the **rudiments** of any specialty in order to excell in it later.
2. When he denounced the church, he was said to be **sacrilegious**.
3. Benjamin Franklin was a **sage** individual who wrote "Poor Richard's Almanac."
4. The **sanctimonious** woman snubbed anyone of whom she disapproved.
5. Attila the Hun is remembered for his **sanguinary** invasion of Europe.
6. The seven-course meal **satiated** my hunger completely.
7. Monty Python is a comedy group noted for its **satires** on daily life.
8. It was so depressing to listen to the **saturnine** professor that few students took his classes.
9. Every election brings out the **schism** that exists within the nation.
10. Prince Charles of England is the **scion** of Queen Elizabeth.
11. Because of his **scrupulous** business practices, he is highly respected.
12. The drunken man is a **scurrilous** rascal.
13. When making beef stew, you should first **sear** the meat in a pan to seal in the juices.
14. He attempted to **secrete** the weapon in his jacket pocket.
15. Those who hold **sedentary** jobs must make a special effort to exercise.
16. **Seismography** is fundamental in the study of California's earthquakes.
17. The old man had become **senile** and could no longer live alone.
18. Very few people can name the U.S. Presidents in the proper **sequence**.
19. "Casper Milquetoast" is the comic portrayal of a **servile** man.
20. When she danced, the lights caused the sequins on her dress to **shimmer**.

But words are things, and a small drop of ink,
Falling, like dew, upon a thought, produces
That which makes thousands, perhaps millions, think.
—Byron, *Don Juan*, canto iii. st. 88.

WORD	DEFINITION	ASSOCIATION *Create and write your associations in the spaces provided!*
1. **rudiment** (roo-di-ment) n.	that which is undeveloped; basic or elementary	______
2. **sacrilegious** (sak-kri-lee-jus) adj.	disrespect to something regarded as sacred	______
3. **sage** (sayj) adj.	wise person; wisdom gained from experience	______
4. **sanctimonious** (sangh-ti-moh-ni-us) adj.	making a show of piety	______
5. **sanguinary** (sang-gwin-ner-ee) adj.	bloodthirsty; bloody; red	______
6. **satiate** (say-shi-ayt) v.	satisfy completely	______
7. **satire** (sat-ir) n.	any use of derisive wit to criticize	______
8. **saturnine** (sat-ur-nin) adj.	gloomy, very serious	See **Saturn** is a very **gloomy** planet.
9. **schism** (sez-em) n.	split or divide in a group, due to differences of opinion	______
10. **scion** (si-on) n.	descendant or heir, esp. noble family	______
11. **scrupulous** (skroo-pyu-lus) adj.	careful; conscientious even in small matters	______
12. **scurrilous** (skur-i-lus) adj.	abusively insulting	______
13. **sear** (seer) v.	scorch or burn with heat; a burning pain	______
14. **secrete** (si-kreet) v.	hide; conceal	______
15. **sedentary** (sed-en-ter-ee) adj.	marked by much sitting or little physical activity	______
16. **seismography** (siz-mog-ra-fee) n.	study of earth vibrations and earthquakes	______
17. **senile** (see-nile) adj.	weak in mind or body, usually from old age	______
18. **sequence** (see-kwens) n.	order in which one thing follows another	______
19. **servile** (sur-vile) adj.	excessively submissive; pertaining to servants	______
20. **shimmer** (shim-er) v.	glimmering light that appears to quiver	______

trib—pay, bestow
See him **trip** as he **pays best-towing** for the work.

WORD ROOT	MEANING	ASSOCIATION *Create and write your associations in the spaces provided!*
TRIB	**pay, bestow**	See him **trip** as he **pays best-towing** for the work.
tribute (trib-yoot) n.	something bestowed as a mark of respect or admiration.	
attribute (a-trib-yoot) v.	to regard as belonging to or caused by.	
contribute (kon-trib-yoot) v.	to give jointly with others.	
distribute (di-strib-yoot) v.	to divide and give a share to each of a number.	
redistribute (ree-dis-trib-yoot) v.	to divide again.	
retribution (ret-ri-byoo-shon) n.	a deserved punishment.	
LIC, LICIT	**permit**	____________________
license (ly-sens) n.	permit from authority to own or do something.	
illicit (i-lis-it) adj.	unlawful, not permitted.	
licentious (ly-sen-shus) adj.	disregarding the rules of conduct.	
licentiate (ly-sen-shi-it) n.	person who holds a certificate showing competency to practice a certain profession.	
unlicensed (un-ly-senst) adj.	having no permit.	
explicit (ik-splis-it) adj.	stating something in exact terms.	
LOQUI, LOC	**speak**	____________________
eloquent (el-o-kwent) adj.	speaking fluently and powerfully.	
loquacious (loh-kway-shus) adj.	talkative.	
soliloquy (so-lil-o-kwee) n.	a speech in which a person expresses his thoughts aloud without addressing any one person.	
obloquy (ob-lo-kwee) n.	verbal abuse.	
interlocutor (in-ter-lok-yu-tor) n.	person who takes part in dialogue.	
elocution (el-o-kyoo-shon) n.	person's style of speaking.	

REVIEW

Draw a line between the word and its correct definition.

1. **seismography**
2. **sanctimonious**
3. **sacrilegious**
4. **retribution**
5. **interlocuter**
6. **scrupulous**
7. **rudiment**
8. **illicit**
9. **saturnine**
10. **satiate**

a. unlawful
b. one who takes part in a dialogue
c. gloomy
d. careful in all matters
e. making a show of piety
f. to satisfy completely
g. deserved punishment
h. disrespect to something sacred
i. a fundamental
j. study of earth vibrations

Circle the correct word below each definition.

1. **abusively insulting**
   (sanguinary, somnolent, sedentary, scurrilous)
2. **use of wit to ridicule**
   (saga, sacrament, satire, scourge)
3. **to conceal**
   (secrete, secede, sequester, simulate)
4. **a split due to difference of opinion**
   (scion, schism, solipsism, specimen)
5. **light that appears to quiver**
   (shinny, shiver, shimmer, shovel)
6. **a descendant**
   (scone, sconce, scion, scintilla)
7. **bloodthirsty**
   (salubrious, salivary, sanguinary, sagacious)
8. **wisdom gained from experience**
   (sagitary, salacious, salient, sage)
9. **excessively submissive**
   (solecistic, servile, somnambulistic, somnolent)
10. **one thing following another**
    (sepulchre, sequence, sequester, seraphic)
11. **to scorch with heat**
    (scowl, scorify, sear, serate)
12. **a life with little physical activity**
    (seditious, sepulchral, sedentary, septenary)
13. **weakness of mind resulting from old age**
    (seminal, semiotic, seneschal, senile)

38

succor (suk-or)—to aid in time of need

See the lost girl given a **sucker** at the **aid** station.

EXAMPLE OF USE

1. The **sociology** professor taught his students about many diverse social institutions.

2. The bombing of Pearl Harbor on 12/7/41 created **solidarity** among the citizens of the United States.

3. One should never take a **soporific** drug before driving a car.

4. The sad movie caused a **spate** of tears in the audience.

5. A high mortality rate is rampant among children who live in **squalor**.

6. Large printing presses are **stationary** to reduce vibration.

7. She wrote the love letter on perfumed **stationery**.

8. He asked for a raise because his **stipend** was so small.

9. "Star Trek's" Mr. Spock is noted for his **stolid** demeanor.

10. From the air, the rows of the cornfield formed **striations** on the land.

11. Clothing that is too tight at the wrists may cause **stricture** of the blood vessels.

12. In a mindless **stupor**, the child sat glued to the TV set.

13. A bruise is caused by slight **subcutaneous** bleeding.

14. The directions on the electric appliance, stated, "Do not **submerge** in water when cleaning."

15. Those who give **succor** to the poor are rewarded with satisfaction—and tax deductions.

16. Juices ran down his chin as he bit into the **succulent** pear.

17. The new company directive **supersedes** the prior one.

18. U.S. **supremacy** in world trade is being challenged by the Japanese.

19. A **surcharge** was imposed in addition to the original purchase price of the home.

20. Good food is life's **sustenance**.

You can forget a blow, but not a word.
—Yiddish proverb

WORD	DEFINITION	ASSOCIATION *Create and write your associations in the spaces provided!*
1. **sociology** (soh-si-ol-o-jee) n.	study of human society and social problems	__________
2. **solidarity** (sol-i-dar-i-tee) n.	unity; oneness of interest	__________
3. **soporific** (sop-o-rif-ik) adj.	drug that induces sleep	__________
4. **spate** (spayt) n.	sudden flood or rush	__________
5. **squalor** (skwol-or) n.	filth and degradation	__________
6. **stationary** (stay-sho-ner-ee) adj.	fixed; not movable	__________
7. **stationery** (stay-sho-ner-ee) n.	writing paper	__________
8. **stipend** (sti-pend) n.	wage; payment at regular intervals	__________
9. **stolid** (stol-id) adj.	unemotional; not excitable	__________
10. **striated** (stai-ay-tid) adj.	marked with narrow lines, bands or ridges	__________
11. **stricture** (strik-chur) n.	restriction; severe criticism	__________
12. **stupor** (stoo-por) n.	daze or extremely apathetic state	__________
13. **subcutaneous** (sub-kyoo-tay-ni-us) adj.	under the skin	__________
14. **submerge** (sub-murj) v.	immerse; put under water or other liquid	__________
15. **succor** (suk-or) v.	to aid in time of need	See the lost girl given a **sucker** at the **aid** station.
16. **succulent** (suk-yu-lent) adj.	juicy; fleshy-tissued	__________
17. **supersede** (soo-per-seed) v.	to supplant; use in place of	__________
18. **supremacy** (soo-prem-a-see) n.	quality of being first in rank or power	__________
19. **surcharge** (sur-chahrj) n.	extra charge or burden	__________
20. **sustenance** (sus-te-nans) n.	means of supporting life; nourishment	__________

gest—carry, bear

See her **carry** the **bear** against her **chest**.

WORD ROOT	MEANING	ASSOCIATION *Create and write your associations in the spaces provided!*
GEST	**carry, bear**	See her **carry** the **bear** against her **chest.**
digest (di-jest) v.	to dissolve food in stomach so it can be absorbed by the body.	
suggest (sug-jest) v.	to propose something for acceptance or rejection.	
congestion (kon-jes-chon) n.	too full, accumulated to excess.	
gesticulate (je-stik-yu-layt) v.	to make expressive movements with the hands and arms.	
gestate (jes-tayt) v.	carry in the womb.	
gesture (jes-chur) n.	an expressive movement of any part of the body.	
TEST	**to bear witness**	____________________
testimony (tes-ti-moh-nee) n.	a declaration or statement under oath.	
protest (proh-test) n.	statement or action showing disapproval of something.	
detest (di-test) v.	to dislike intensely.	
contest (kon-test) v.	to dispute or challenge.	
attest (a-test) v.	to declare to be true or genuine.	
testament (tes-ta-ment) n.	a written statement of one's beliefs.	
MITT, MISS	**send**	____________________
mission (mish-on) n.	envoys sent to a foreign country.	
commit (ko-mit) v.	to do, to perform.	
submit (sub-mit) v.	to present for consideration or decision.	
emit (i-mit) v.	to send out.	
remiss (ri-mis) adj.	negligent.	
emissary (em-i-ser-ee) n.	person sent to conduct negotiations.	

REVIEW

Mark true or false in the space provided.

1. ________ An **emissary** is a person sent to conduct negotiations.
2. ________ A **stolid** individual has a powerful build.
3. ________ To **gestate** is to make expressive movements with one's hands.
4. ________ **Squalor** is a state of filth and deprivation.
5. ________ A **soporific** reaction is what you'd expect from someone childish.
6. ________ A **spate** of criticism is a sudden flood of bad news.
7. ________ **Stationary** is stylized writing paper.
8. ________ To **contest** a decision is to vocally disagree.
9. ________ Greek temples are often supported by **striated** columns.
10. ________ A **stipend** is a ticket presented for violation of a law.

Mark the letter from column 2 that best describes each word in column 1.

1	2
sustenance ________	a. study of human social problems
submerge ________	b. writing paper
sociology ________	c. apathetic state
stationery ________	d. put under water
stricture ________	e. to aid in time of need
subcutaneous ________	f. juicy
succor ________	g. first in rank
supersede ________	h. under the skin
solidarity ________	i. adverse criticism
supremacy ________	j. oneness of interest
surcharge ________	k. means of supporting life
stupor ________	l. to use in place of
succulent ________	m. an additional amount of money

tabloid (tab-loid)—newspaper of small page size
See on the **table odd** and **small-sized newspapers**.

39

EXAMPLE OF USE

1. I felt **sympathy** for her in her grief.

2. **Synchronize** your watches, and meet me back here exactly at eight.

3. "Here" is a **synonym** for "at this place."

4. The *National Enquirer* is a **tabloid**.

5. A race car's rpm is measured by a **tachometer**.

6. The sightless person uses his **tactile** sense to read Braille.

7. For some people music is **tantamount** to ecstasy.

8. Children seem to enjoy **taunting** each other.

9. The rock concert presented a challenge to the police because of the **teeming** crowds.

10. I didn't have the time to send a letter, so I sent a **telegram**.

11. No one knows how a mental **telepathist** is able to read minds.

12. Kitt Peak National Observatory in Arizona has one of the world's largest **telescopes**.

13. The lawyer had the **temerity** to make irresponsible accusations in court.

14. Political campaigns invariably produce **tendentious** literature.

15. Too many drugs can give a person a **tenuous** hold on reality.

16. He made a good map of the **terrain**.

17. Her **terse** manner of speaking made some people think she had little to say.

18. He is a **theology** student at the seminary.

19. They are compatible friends, for one is bold and the other is **timorous**.

20. The overcast sky showed a **tinge** of blue, so we knew that tomorrow's weather would be clear.

I never desire to converse with a man who has written more than he has read.
—Samuel Johnson

WORD	DEFINITION	ASSOCIATION *Create and write your associations in the spaces provided!*
1. **sympathy** (sim-pa-thee) n.	harmony of feeling or thought	______
2. **synchronize** (sin-kro-niz) v.	occur or exist at the same time	______
3. **synonym** (sin-o-nim) n.	word with same or similar meaning as another word	______
4. **tabloid** (tab-loid) n.	newspaper of small page size	See on the **table odd** and **small-sized** newspapers.
5. **tachometer** (ta-kom-e-ter) n.	instrument for measuring speed of rotation	______
6. **tactile** (tak-til) adj.	using the sense of touch	______
7. **tantamount** (tan-ta-mount) adj.	equivalent	______
8. **taunt** (tawnt) v.	reproach in mocking or insulting manner	______
9. **teeming** (teem-ing) v.	overcrowded; abundant	______
10. **telegram** (tel-e-gram) n.	message transmitted across distances	______
11. **telepathy** (te-lap-e-thee) n.	psychic transmission of ideas	______
12. **telescope** (tel-e-skohp) n.	device that enlarges the images of distant objects	______
13. **temerity** (te-mer-i-tee) n.	recklessness; rash boldness	______
14. **tendentious** (ten-den-shus) adj.	prejudiced; biased; aimed at helping a cause	______
15. **tenuous** (ten-yoo-us) adj.	fragile; frail; slight	______
16. **terrain** (te-rayn) n.	geographical characteristics of an area of land	______
17. **terse** (turs) adj.	clipped; to the point; curt	______
18. **theology** (thi-ol-o-jee) n.	study of religion	______
19. **timorous** (tim-o-rus) adj.	easily frightened; hesitant; timid	______
20. **tinge** (tinj) v.	hint; trace	______

eu—well, good
See the **'U'** painted on the **good** side of the **well**.

WORD ROOT	MEANING	ASSOCIATION *Create and write your associations in the spaces provided!*
EU	**well, good**	See the **'U'** painted on the **good** side of the **well.**
euphonious (yoo-foh-ni-us) adj.	pleasing sounds.	
eulogy (yoo-lo-jee) n.	speech or writing in praise of someone.	
euphoria (yoo-fohr-i-a) n.	a feeling of general well-being.	
eureka (yuu-ree-ka) interj.	"I have found it!"—exclaimed at discovery.	
eugenics (yoo-jen-iks) n.	study of improvement of human species by improvement of inherited qualities.	
euthanasia (yoo-tha-nay-zha) n.	bringing about of a gentle and easy death for a person suffering from a painful incurable disease.	
ANTE	**before**	______________________
antebellum (an-ti-bel-um) adj.	before the war.	
antecedent (an-ti-see-dant) n.	thing or circumstance that came before.	
anteroom (an-ti-room) n.	room leading to a more important one.	
anterior (an-teer-i-or) adj.	coming before in time or position.	
antediluvian (an-ti-di-loo-vi-an) adj.	of the time before the Flood.	
antedate (an-ti-dayt) v.	to put an earlier date on.	
ACER, ACRI	**bitter, sour, sharp**	______________________
acid (as-id) adj.	sharp tasting, sour.	
acerbate (as-er-bayt) v.	to make sour or bitter.	
acrid (ak-rid) adj.	having a bitter smell or taste.	
acrimony (ak-ri-moh-nee) n.	bitterness of manner or words.	
acidemia (as-i-dee-meea) n.	condition of too much acid in the blood.	
acidimeter (as-i-dim-e-ter) n.	instrument to measure amount of acid.	

REVIEW

Mark the letter of the correct word for each definition in the space provided.

1. **psychic transmission of thoughts**
   a. temerity b. telepathy c. tirade ________
2. **instrument for measuring speed of rotation**
   a. tabernacle b. tachistoscope c. tachometer ________
3. **the act of allowing an incurably ill person to die at will**
   a. eugenics b. euphoria c. euthanasia ________
4. **to make bitter**
   a. aggregate b. acerbate c. agglutinate ________
5. **referring to before the war**
   a. antediluvian b. antecedent c. antebellum ________
6. **a word with a definition similar to another**
   a. synapse b. synonym c. antonym ________
7. **a small newspaper with many pictures**
   a. tableau b. tabard c. tabloid ________
8. **study of religion**
   a. theomachy b. theocracy c. theology ________
9. **the quality of being easily frightened**
   a. tinctorial b. timorous c. tempestuous ________
10. **advancing a specific point of view**
    a. tenebrific b. tenuous c. tendentious ________

Mark the letter or write the word that best completes each sentence.

1. To be sure that we're both on time, let's ____________ our watches.
   a. synergize b. synchronize c. syllogize
2. Appreciation of sculpture usually involves the ____________ sense.
   a. tactical b. tacit c. tactile
3. When a person dies, it is customary to express one's ____________ to surviving members of the family.
   a. symmetry b. sympathy c. synecdoche
4. She no longer has even a ____________ of self-pity.
   a. tinge b. tirl c. tithe
5. The students' arguments for more freedoms were ____________ at best.
   a. teleological b. tensile c. tenuous
6. Working for minimum wage is ____________ to slavery.
   a. tantamount b. paramount c. tandem
7. The news of a new assignment came by ____________.
   a. telescope b. telegram c. teleology
8. It is virtually impossible to land a plane in rugged ____________.
   a. tenure b. terrine c. terrain
9. Responding to the hecklers, the president gave a ____________ reply.
   a. tertiary c. terse c. thalassic
10. The most valuable instrument for an astronomer is the ____________.
    a. telescope b. telegram c. telephone
11. The young boy had the ____________ to ask me how old I am.
    a. tenacity b. temerity c. tensibility
12. The air is ____________ with insects during the summer.
    a. teeming b. theming c. thwarting
13. It was the bully's nature to ____________ the others to violence.
    a. thaw b. taut c. taunt

titanic (ti-tan-ik)—gigantic
The S.S. **Titanic** was **gigantic**!

EXAMPLE OF USE

1. It was a **titanic** struggle between the forces of good and evil.

2. The smell of her perfume **titillates** my senses.

3. We checked the **topography** of the area before starting out on our camping trip.

4. The **tortuous** road wound through the mountain pass.

5. Her ambition to become an actress **transcends** all her other desires in her life.

6. The movie theater audience was **transfixed** by the horror movie.

7. Many **transients** find work as field hands as they pass through the area.

8. She **transmitted** the memo to the chairman of the board.

9. Her fear of flying caused her to approach the airplane with **trepidation**.

10. Because she speaks English, French, and German she works as a **trilingual** interpreter.

11. *Lord of the Rings* is a well-known **trilogy**.

12. The photographer attached his camera to the **tripod** before starting the photo session.

13. Many people fear Friday the 13th—this is called **triskaidekaphobia**.

14. Why are we arguing over such a **trivial** matter?

15. "Haste makes waste" is a **truism**.

16. The student required additional **tutelage** in order to pass his SAT exam.

17. His father presented him with an **ultimatum** to try to force him to behave.

18. I take **umbrage** at your insults.

19. His **unbridled** rage drove him to lunge at his tormentor.

20. You have just stated an **unequivocal** truth!

If you don't say anything, you won't be called on to repeat it.
—Calvin Coolidge

WORD	DEFINITION	ASSOCIATION *Create and write your associations in the spaces provided!*
1. **titanic** (ti-tan-ik) adj.	gigantic	The S.S. **Titanic** was **gigantic**!
2. **titillate** (tit-i-layt) v.	evoke a pleasurable response	________
3. **topography** (to-pog-ra-fee) n.	physical characteristics of a given terrain	________
4. **tortuous** (tor-choo-us) adj.	full of twists and turns; devious	________
5. **transcend** (tran-send) v.	rise above; excel; surpass	________
6. **transfix** (trans-fiks) v.	pierce; to impale; make motionless with fear	________
7. **transient** (tran-shent) n.	one who passes through or stays temporarily; migrant	________
8. **transmit** (trans-mit) v.	convey; transfer; pass along	________
9. **trepidation** (trep-i-day-shon) n.	fear; dread; apprehension	________
10. **trilingual** (tri-ling-gwal) adj.	speaking or using three languages	________
11. **trilogy** (tril-o-jee) n.	literary or dramatic work produced in three parts	________
12. **tripod** (tri-pod) n.	three-legged contrivance intended to hold something	________
13. **triskaidekaphobia** (tris-ka-dek-a-foh-bee-ah) n.	unsubstantiated fear of the number thirteen	________
14. **trivial** (triv-i-al) adj.	of small value or importance	________
15. **truism** (troo-iz-em) n.	trite statement; hackneyed phrase	________
16. **tutelage** (too-ta-lij) n.	teaching; instruction	________
17. **ultimatum** (ul-ti-may-tum) n.	final demand of condition	________
18. **umbrage** (um-brij) n.	to take offense	________
19. **unbridled** (un-bri-deld) adj.	unrestrained	________
20. **unequivocal** (un-i-kwiv-o-kal) adj.	unmistakable; without a doubt	________

pneumon, pneuma—breath

He feels like a **new man breathing** in the fresh air.

WORD ROOT	MEANING	ASSOCIATION *Create and write your associations in the spaces provided!*
PNEUMON, PNEUMA	**breath**	He feels like a **new man breathing** in the fresh air.
pneumonia (nuu-mohn-ya) n.	inflammation of one or both lungs.	
pneumoconiosis (noo-moh-koh-ni-oh-sis) n.	lung disease caused by inhalation of dust.	
MORT, MORS	**death**	________________
mortal (mor-tal) adj.	subject to death.	
moribund (mor-i-bund) adj.	in a dying state.	
SYN	**with, together**	________________
synopsis (si-nop-sis) n.	a summary, brief general survey.	
synthesis (sin-the-sis) n.	combining of separate parts or elements to form a complex whole.	
ENDO	**within**	________________
endogenous (en-doj-e-nus) adj.	growing or originating from within.	
endocrine (en-do-krin) adj.	(a gland) pouring its secretions straight into the blood.	
CATA, CAT	**down, completely**	________________
catastrophe (ka-tas-tro-fee) n.	a sudden great disaster.	
cataract (kat-a-ract) n.	condition in the lens of the eye—breaks down and becomes cloudy and obscures sight.	
ANA	**up, upon, again**	________________
analogy (a-nal-o-jee) n.	a partial likeness between two things compared.	
anagram (an-a-gram) n.	a word or phrase formed from the rearranged letters in another.	

REVIEW

Draw a line between the word and its correct definition.

1. **unequivocal**	a. full of twists and turns
2. **trivial**	b. fear
3. **umbrage**	c. of little importance
4. **tutelage**	d. final demand of conditions
5. **tortuous**	e. instruction
6. **titanic**	f. to take offense
7. **transmit**	g. trite statement
8. **titillate**	h. to rise above
9. **truism**	i. evoke a pleasurable response
10. **unbridled**	j. gigantic
11. **ultimatum**	k. to convey information
12. **trepidation**	l. unmistakable
13. **transcend**	m. unrestrained

Circle the correct word below each definition.

1. **unsubstantiated fear of the number thirteen**
   (trichinosis, triskaidekaphobia, trichotomous, triforium)
2. **in a dying state**
   (mordant, morbid, moribund, mortification)
3. **literary work produced in three parts**
   (trinary, trimester, tribunal, trilogy)
4. **a word formed by rearranging the letters to spell another word**
   (assimilation, amalgamation, anagram, anachronism)
5. **physical characteristics of a certain terrain**
   (typography, topography, tortuosity, traction)
6. **someone who stays in one place temporarily**
   (transept, transliterate, transient, transparency)
7. **a brief, general survey of a subject**
   (synapse, synopsis, system, synonym)
8. **three-legged base on which other instruments are supported**
   (trituration, triptych, tripartite, tripod)
9. **to make motionless**
   (transubstantiate, transfigure, transfix, transcribe)
10. **speaking three languages**
    (tributary, trident, trilingual, trierarchy)

41

untenable (un-ten-a-bel)—(a theory) will not hold—
argument can be made against it

Picture someone **unable to hold** onto an **antenna**.

EXAMPLE OF USE

1. Even his closest friends find his reasons for moving **unfathomable**.
2. Her **unfurrowed** face belied her age.
3. Common interests help **unify** a group.
4. We were dismayed to see his dirty, **unkempt** appearance.
5. Your argument is **untenable** because I can prove the world is round.
6. The father found it necessary to **upbraid** his naughty son.
7. Many people think "Bigfoot" is a bear because of its **ursine** appearance.
8. Interest rates are set by the government to prevent **usury**.
9. Some people spend their lives looking for **utopia**.
10. He proposed to her, but she **vacillated** before giving her answer.
11. In an old-time melodrama, the hero always **vanquishes** the villain in the story.
12. The Zoning Commission was hesitant to grant the zone **variance** because of the effect the change would have on the community.
13. When a car comes toward you, reflex causes you to **veer** away from it.
14. It's not unusual to feel **vehement** hatred for one's enemies.
15. In the time of Dickens, writers were **verbose** because they were paid by the word.
16. The priest donned his **vestment** before conducting Mass.
17. Both alternatives are **viable**, but the first would be easier to carry out.
18. The two contestants **vied** for the office of class president.
19. Instead of being grateful for the help, the man proved to be **viperous** toward his benefactor.
20. The poison of the rattlesnake is **virulent** and can cause death.

Oratory: the art of making deep noises from the chest sound like important messages from the brain.
—H.J. Phillips

WORD	DEFINITION	ASSOCIATION *Create and write your associations in the spaces provided!*
1. **unfathomable** (un-fath-um-ah-bel) adj.	too deep to be measured; incomprehensible	______
2. **unfurrowed** (un-fur-rowd) adj.	smooth	______
3. **unify** (yoo-ni-fy) v.	to bring together; unite	______
4. **unkempt** (un-kempt) adj.	untidy; disheveled	______
5. **untenable** (un-ten-a-bel) adj.	will not hold—argument can be made against it	Picture someone **unable to hold** onto an **antenna.**
6. **upbraid** (up-brayd) v.	reproach with severity; scold	______
7. **ursine** ((ur-sine) adj.	pertaining to a bear; bearlike	______
8. **usury** (yoo-zhu-ree) n.	lending of money at excessive interest rate	______
9. **utopia** (yoo-toh-pi-a) n.	imaginary, ideal state where everything is perfect	______
10. **vacillate** (vas-i-layt) v.	hesitate; waver; fluctuate	______
11. **vanquish** (vang-kwish) v.	overcome; conquer; defeat	______
12. **variance** (vair-i-ans) n.	state of being different or in disagreement	______
13. **veer** (veer) v.	shift or change direction	______
14. **vehement** (vee-e-ment) adj.	passionate; characterized by strong feelings	______
15. **verbose** (ver-bohs) adj.	using more words than needed	______
16. **vestment** (vest-ment) n.	ceremonial robe or other garment	______
17. **viable** (vi-a-bel) adj.	capable of developing; able to live or grow	______
18. **vie** (vi) v.	compete; strive for superiority	______
19. **viperous** (vi-per-us) adj.	spiteful; person who betrays one who has helped him	______
20. **virulent** (vir-yu-lent) adj.	actively poisonous; bitterly hostile	______

poly—many
See **Poly** wants **many** crackers!

WORD ROOT	MEANING	ASSOCIATION *Create and write your associations in the spaces provided!*
POLY	**many**	See **Poly** wants **many** crackers!
polyhedron (pol-ee-hee-dron) n.	a solid figure with many faces (usually seven or more).	
polyglot (pol-ee-glot) n.	person who knows several languages.	
ABLE	**having power**	______________________
enjoyable (en-joi-a-bel) adj.	giving enjoyment, pleasant.	
agreeable (a-gree-a-bel) adj.	pleasing, willing to agree.	
PRE	**before**	______________________
precaution (pri-kaw-shon) n.	something done in advance to avoid a risk.	
prejudice (prej-u-dis) n.	an unreasonable opinion or like or dislike of something.	
IN	**in, within, into, not**	______________________
inhale (in-hayl) v.	to breathe in, to draw into the lungs by breathing.	
inability (in-a-bill-i-tee) n.	being unable.	
POST	**after, behind, later**	______________________
postscript (pohst-skript) n.	a paragraph added at the end of something (especially a letter).	
post mortem (pohst-mortem) n.	an examination made after death to determine its cause.	
JUXT	**near, next**	______________________
juxtapose (juk-sta-pohz) v.	to put things side by side.	
juxtaposition (juk-sta-pe-zish-un) n.	parallel objects or ideas.	

REVIEW

Mark true or false in the space provided.

1. ________ A **juxtaposition** is two things presented side by side.
2. ________ To be **virulent** is to have a high fever.
3. ________ A **polyhedron** is someone who only sees god in people.
4. ________ An **untenable** position is one that cannot be argued against.
5. ________ A **utopia** is a perfect, and therefore imaginary, state.
6. ________ A **prejudice** is an opinion prejudged before one tries to understand.
7. ________ A **vestment** is money set aside for a specific purpose.
8. ________ To **vacillate** between decisions involves hesitation.
9. ________ To **upbraid** someone is to help them climb up.
10. ________ A state of **variance** is one of disagreement.

Mark the letter from column 2 that best describes each word in column 1.

1		2
viperous	________	a. spiteful
unkempt	________	b. to overcome
unfathomable	________	c. bearlike
unify	________	d. untidy
ursine	________	e. too deep to be measured
vanquish	________	f. smooth
veer	________	g. to shift direction
viable	________	h. able to develop
unfurrowed	________	i. using more words than needed
verbose	________	j. to compete
vehement	________	k. lending money for interest fee
vie	________	l. with strong feeling
usury	________	m. to bring together

vogue (vohg)—current fashion or trend 42

Vogue magazine reports the **current** popular **fashion**.

EXAMPLE OF USE

1. The poet is quite a **visionary**.
2. She was so **vivacious** that she livened up the party.
3. Short hair is now in **vogue**, say the fashion experts.
4. He decided of his own **volition** to go to the party.
5. A tornado is an example of a **vortex**.
6. He is a clever businessman and runs the business in a **vulpine** manner.
7. The child was **wan** from being ill for so long.
8. Try not to **warp** the truth!
9. The child tried to **wheedle** a "yes" from his mother.
10. She bought the high-fashion jeans on a **whim**.
11. Even grownups enjoy that **whirligig** at the amusement park.
12. During inspection, the army officer would not permit a **whit** of dust.
13. After seeing the romantic movie, her face developed a **wistful** look.
14. He is **wont** to go jogging every day.
15. Losing his job has brought him to **wrack** and ruin.
16. The two waiters **wrangled** over who deserved the tip left on the table.
17. The **yannigan** was hoping to make the major league team.
18. I have a **yen** to go to Paris.
19. He loved being a **zany** member of the circus.
20. The night's **zephyr** gently rustled the leaves on the trees.

It is astonishing what power words have over man.
—Napoleon Bonaparte

WORD	DEFINITION	ASSOCIATION *Create and write your associations in the spaces provided!*
1. **visionary** (vizh-o-ner-ee) adj.	dreamer; one who is impractical	________
2. **vivacious** (vi-vay-shus) adj.	lively; high spirited	________
3. **vogue** (vohg) n.	current fashion or trend	**Vogue** magazine reports the **current** popular **fashion**.
4. **volition** (vo-lish-on) n.	will; choosing one's own decision	________
5. **vortex** (vor-taks) n.	whirlpool; something resembling a whirlpool	________
6. **vulpine** (vul-pine) adj.	cunning; crafty; foxlike	________
7. **wan** (wan) adj.	colorless; pale	________
8. **warp** (worp) v.	bend, turn or twist out of shape; falsify	________
9. **wheedle** (hwee-del) v.	gain by flattery or coaxing	________
10. **whim** (hwim) n.	a sudden unreasonable desire or impulse	________
11. **whirligig** (wur-le-gig) n.	something that spins around (as a top or carousel)	________
12. **whit** (hwit) n.	smallest part; jot	________
13. **wistful** (wist-ful) adj.	wishful; full of sad or vague longing	________
14. **wont** (wohnt) adj.	habit; practice; custom	________
15. **wrack** (rak) n.	wreck or wreckage; ruin	________
16. **wrangle** (rang-gel) v.	angry dispute or noisy quarrel; altercation	________
17. **yannigan** (yan-e-gen) n.	member of a scrub team in baseball	________
18. **yen** (yen) n.	longing; yearning	________
19. **zany** (zay-nee) n.	clown or buffoon; ludicrously comical	________
20. **zephyr** (zef-ir) n.	soft, gentle breeze	________

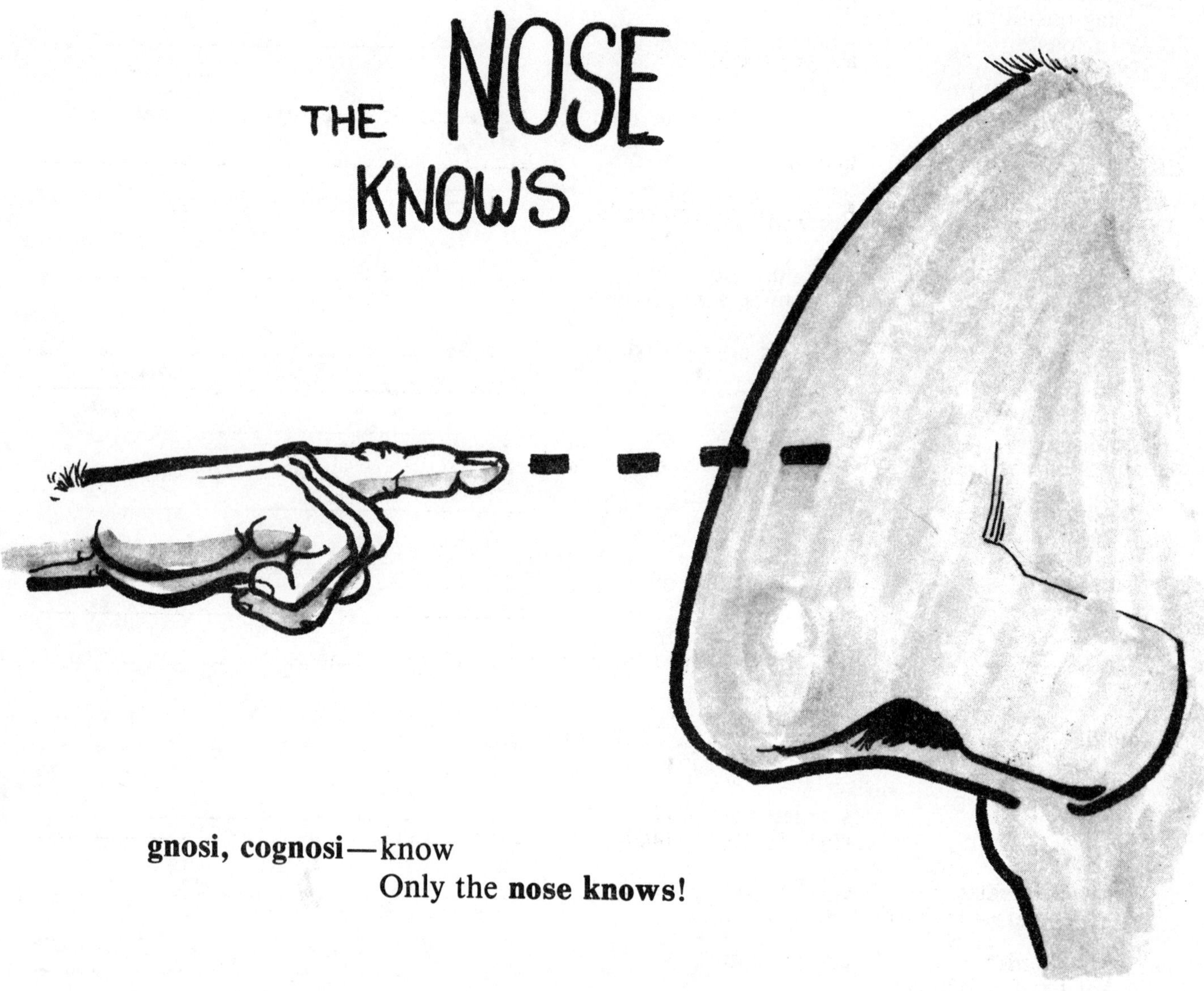

gnosi, cognosi—know

Only the **nose knows**!

WORD ROOT	MEANING	ASSOCIATION *Create and write your associations in the spaces provided!*
GNOSI, COGNOSI	**know**	Only the **nose knows**!
agnostic (ag-nos-tik) n.	person who believes that nothing can be known of God's existence.	
cognition (kog-nish-on) n.	act or process of knowing.	
CRED	**believe**	______________________
credulity (kre-doo-li-tee) n.	believe things too readily.	
incredible (in-kred-i-bel) adj.	unbelievable.	
LAUD	**praise**	______________________
laudable (law-da-bel) adj.	praiseworthy.	
laudatory (law-da-thor-ee) adj.	praising.	
NOV	**new**	______________________
innovate (in-o-vayt) v.	to introduce a new process or way of doing things.	
novice (nov-is) n.	a beginner.	
ORTHO	**correct, right, straight**	______________________
orthochromatic (or-tho-kro-mat-ik)adj.	correct color.	
orthophonic (or-tho-fawn-ik) adj.	correct sound.	
LUCR	**gain, profit**	______________________
lucrative (loo-kra-tiv) adj.	profitable, money making.	
lucre (loo-ker) n.	(contemptuous) money, money making as a motive for action.	

REVIEW

Mark the letter of the correct word for each definition in the space provided.

1. **something that spins around**
   a. wheedle b. whirligig c. whoopdedo ________
2. **a state of ruin**
   a. wisteria b. wrack c. willy-nilly ________
3. **acting of one's own free will**
   a. volatile b. vitriolic c. volition ________
4. **someone who doubts that man can know about God's existence**
   a. apostle b. arbiter c. agnostic ________
5. **to introduce a new way of doing things**
   a. invocate b. innovate c. induct ________
6. **a cunning and crafty nature**
   a. vulnerable b. voluptuous c. vulpine ________
7. **an action that deserves praise**
   a. laudable b. languorous c. lamentable ________
8. **a dreamer with impractical ideas**
   a. vicar b. valedictorian c. visionary ________
9. **something resembling a whirlpool**
   a. vortex b. vignette c. virtuoso ________
10. **member of a scrub team in baseball**
    a. yankee b. yannigan c. yeshiva ________

Mark the letter or write the word that best completes each sentence.

1. Marilyn Monroe was known as a __________ blonde in her films.
   a. vicarious b. vivacious c. vigilant
2. There is no way that he will ever __________ the secret out of me.
   a. waver b. wheeze c. wheedle
3. The Japanese have the __________ to travel.
   a. yonder b. yen c. yawl
4. He jumped in the car and drove 500 miles on a __________.
   a. wiseacre b. whim c. whiff
5. As they rested on the balcony, a __________ blew in from the West.
   a. zeitgeist b. zephyr c. zwieback
6. Every year several people at the office party __________ over politics.
   a. wheedle b. wobble c. wrangle
7. Comedians tend to present an exceptionally __________ picture of life.
   a. zodiacal b. zany c. zymotic
8. Leaving wood out in the rain is apt to __________ the surface.
   a. warp b. wean c. whimper
9. People who are dying usually have a __________ expression.
   a. waif b. wan c. whet
10. At this company, people can adjust their starting time as is their __________.
    a. wastrel b. wassail c. wont
11. I assure you, I don't care a __________ about the outcome.
    a. whig b. whit c. whisk
12. Listening to Gregorian chants is not currently in __________.
    a. vichy b. vacuity c. vogue
13. Looking at a scrapbook of pictures from her childhood gave her a __________ feeling.
    a. willful b. wistful c. wimple

WORD INDEX

g

h

i

WORD ROOT INDEX

PREFIXES & SUFFIXES

WORD ROOTS